SELLING BY THE NUMBERS

SELLING BY THE NUMBERS

Jason C. Miller

iUniverse, Inc.
New York   Lincoln   Shanghai

Selling by the Numbers

iUniverse, Inc.

For information address:
iUniverse, Inc.
2021 Pine Lake Road, Suite 100
Lincoln, NE 68512
www.iuniverse.com

ISBN: 0-595-32688-9 (Pbk)
ISBN: 0-595-66666-3 (Cloth)

Printed in the United States of America

Contents

Acknowledgements

I take credit for assembling this approach and for taking the time to commit it to paper. I do not take credit for creating it. Everything I know I've learned over the last twenty-five years from watching hundreds of salespeople wrestle with the craft. I've learned more from the ones that did it wrong than I did from the ones who did it right. More importantly, having worked with so many different salespeople over such a large geography, I have been able to identify common threads. I've gained a tremendous respect for those rare few who have truly mastered the art.

To all those salespeople who knowingly or unknowingly have contributed to my learning curve, I offer my deepest gratitude. I hope that I can use what I've learned from each of you to make life more exciting for the many salespeople who have not yet experienced the splendor that a career in selling has to offer.

I'm also grateful to my former boss, Art. With no small amount of pain, I grew more as a businessman under his tutelage than anyone I had worked with before or since. He was a most unlikely influence early in my selling career. Buried among the hundreds of sentence sermons were two inescapable tenets. First, "Good enough rarely is," and second, "Right is right even if no one is doing it, wrong is wrong even if everyone is doing it."

More than any single person, I would like to recognize my wife's role in this book and in my career. She's my best friend and partner for life. We all face individual moments of truth, character-defining moments when you feel like you just can't do it. Since my late teen years, there has been one person who always knew deep down that I would overcome any obstacle in my way. She believed in me even when I had trouble believing in myself. Throughout this book, you will feel my core belief: I am capable of achieving any goal to which I set my mind. To my wife, for this most important character trait, I am eternally grateful and completely indebted. And I thank my two beautiful daughters. In their presence I feel like a hero. Regardless of how tough life would get, all I needed to do was look into their precious eyes for the inspiration to blast through any obstacles and become all that I could be. If you are not surrounding yourself with people who believe in you even when it's tough to believe in yourself, you will never experience the joy and power that has guided my life.

—*Jason C. Miller*

Introduction

Have you noticed how many books have been written about selling? If you've read them, you might be surprised at how different each approach is. Why is that? As the "oldest profession," you'd think by now that someone would have figured it out and explained it in simple terms. Selling, like any other profession, has a set of skills that must be learned to be effective.

The reason for all these approaches is fairly simple. Selling requires creativity, enthusiasm, ingenuity, intuition, interpretation, and perception. Whereas an effective salesperson must be a detective; an ambassador; a consultant; a teacher; and a psychiatrist, sales champions are artists. Selling is more of an art form than a skill, so there is no single right way to do it. Learning to be an artist is no small challenge.

As a young man, I wished I could create beautiful painting like the ones I had seen in galleries. Even though I am fairly artistic by nature, I could have all the right paints and all the right brushes, but I simply could not get the right colors in the right places to create what I saw in my mind's eye. I remember watching a television show on PBS; it was a show designed to teach people how to paint. I don't remember the artist's name. All I can remember is this big brush he would call the "mighty brush." Every time he wielded it and attacked the canvas, I was convinced he was destroying the picture. Somehow, miraculously, the rest of the colors fell into place, and the result was downright unbelievable. Watch the show a few times, and you'll realize that there are basic principles behind every stroke. Once you understand them, the mystery fades. Only then can you venture out and create your own paintings with greater confidence and competence.

That's how you "learn" an art. You must learn the basics and understand how they fit together before you can create your own style. Too many selling books try to teach a specific style. Because there are as many styles of selling as there are salespeople, there are potentially an infinite number of books that can be written on the subject. Most salespeople will read one or more of these books and pick out at least one or two tips that fit their style. Their approach becomes a patchwork of styles that may provide some level of success but never really helps the salesperson master the craft.

Selling by the Numbers breaks the process into individual components and tells you how to fill them in. Once you understand each component in the process, you can use that understanding to develop your own style. Whether you're new to sales or revitalizing a stagnant career, this book can help. You must, however, resist the temptation to second-guess or challenge the approach when it doesn't match your current approach. If your current approach were everything you'd ever hoped it would be, you would not be reading this book.

Like any art form, it's not something that you learn one day and just start doing. Each day and each customer is a blank canvas that will present new challenges and new opportunities. Some will be magnificent, some not so magnificent. A few may be downright ugly. Once you embrace the basics, however, successes are easier to repeat, and pure failures disappear. Your highs will be higher and more frequent. Your lows will not be as low, and they will be rare.

1

What's the Point?

*Progress must be measured from the peak,
not the trailhead.*

Before you do anything, you must be crystal clear about what you're trying to achieve. If you aren't, you'll waste a lot of time wandering around until you figure it out. Once you know precisely what you're trying to accomplish, you will plainly see whether all the craziness you engage in during the day is helping you to get there.

What is the purpose of a company?

Ask this question to people from the top ranks to the bottom, and you are likely to get one of two predictable responses:

1. To make a profit.
2. To produce and distribute a certain combination of goods or services.

If you believe that making a profit is the purpose of your company, I feel badly for you. Profit is never the purpose of an organization; it is only a goal at best. It's a kind of scorecard. Don't misunderstand, profit is critically important if a company is to continue to access the resources needed to accomplish its purpose. If profit is the purpose of a company, how do you explain not-for-profit organizations? Some of the most important contributions to our quality of life are provided by organizations structured never to generate a profit. Furthermore, even the most robust and successful organizations go through periods of difficulty earning a profit.

The CF Story

At one time or another, many of us have driven past a Consolidated Freightways truck. With tens of thousands of trucks and trailers hauling freight to hundreds of terminals across the country, it is hard to drive in this country without passing at least one. At least, that would have been the case prior to Labor Day, 2002. Today CF no longer exists.

Its demise had haunted me for two solid years, and I couldn't figure out why. On the surface, I was saddened for the thousands of great people working for CF who had lost their jobs. Yet I knew my anxiety was related to something more than that because I found myself more focused on the demise of CF than on the individuals I knew.

CF was a powerhouse, an innovator, and an icon. The story begins in 1929 in Portland, Oregon. A young man named Leland James began a small company hauling freight. No truck manufacturer at the time built a truck powerful enough, long enough, and light enough to effectively haul freight to the west coast, across the Rocky Mountains. Instead of complaining, he developed one. Once his truck was proven effective, he built a few more, giving them the name *Freightliner*. By the late 1940s, Freightliners were being produced and sold to other companies. In the decades that followed, Consolidated Freightways, founded by James, became one of the nation's largest trucking companies, while Freightliner became one of the largest truck manufacturers in the world.

Okay, a big company goes broke and goes away. It's not like it's the first time that's happened. So why does it haunt me? Was it because I knew dozens of people who worked there? In hindsight, I'm sorry to say that we never met socially other than the occasional business lunch. I knew very little of their personal lives and shared little of my own. No, my angst was tied to something deeper and much more troubling.

What, exactly, is the point to all of this? That was the real question. After all, I just sell tires. If I weren't here tomorrow to sell these tires, would it really make a difference? I once read that if you want to see how replaceable you are, stick your fist into a pail of water, yank it out fast and notice how long it takes for the water to fill the hole. Every time I asked myself that question, I could not help but reflect on those people I knew at CF. They went to work each day believing they made a difference. They knew that the company they worked for had invented most of the trucks on the road. Furthermore, the lion's share of the products on the shelves were there either because a CF truck driver delivered them or because another carrier delivered them with a Freightliner truck, which was initially created by Leland James. When CF people went to work each day, they had a clear answer to the question, "What's the point?"

I can't count how many drivers, mechanics, foremen, managers, executives and salespeople I met in my 20+ years' experience with CF. Many joined CF right out of high school or college and never even considered working somewhere else. Some were second-generation CF employees. Many had been offered higher paying positions with other companies, but they were too loyal to even consider leaving. Not loyal by today's standards but rather by a deeper standard that no longer exists. Loyal like the stories we would hear from our great grandfathers. They weren't co-workers. They were a family!

Then on Monday, September 2, 2002 (ironically it was Labor Day), thousands of CF employees showed up to work only to be greeted by locked gates and security guards. The following is a description of the final few weeks as described to me by a now displaced former CF employee who I considered a friend. A few of the branch managers were allowed in and escorted to their offices by security guards. They were told, and I'm not exaggerating, "Call me if you need to use the restroom, I'll escort you. Then call me when you're ready to leave for the day, we'll escort you out. You might consider bringing lunch with you to work, we don't want a lot of coming and going." Once at their desks, they received a call informing them that the company was being liquidated and that they wanted a select few to remain while they closed the company and liquidated the assets. "Oh, by the way, if you choose not to stay, it will be considered a voluntary separation, which may jeopardize your ability to collect unemployment. Furthermore, insurance was cancelled effective the prior day, and since it is tied up in bankruptcy court, you may or may not see timely payment for the days worked while liquidating!"

Then, in the blink of an eye, CF was gone forever. A rogue entrepreneur was trying to corral some investors in a futile attempt to buy the assets and restore some semblance of the company, but those rumblings have since subsided, and most of the locations and equipment have been sold. I have not yet shared what is, at least for me, the most troubling aspect of this story. It's not the demise. It's the fact that just a few years later, it's almost as if the company never existed! I manage a tire company and, less than a year ago, hired a new salesman. During his initial orientation I was sharing stories about doing business with CF. He looked at me, a bit confused and said, "Who?" I said, "CF, you know, Consolidated Freightways?" To which he replied, "Oh yeah, I think I've heard of them." And that's it. It's now folklore. How do you go from historic, groundbreaking powerhouse to folklore? If it can happen to them, what makes us think it couldn't happen to any of us? And, if it could just as easily happen to any of us, what exactly is the point to all this energy and passion that we invest in our careers each day? Is it, really, just a job? And do we really need to answer this question?

We do need to answer this question and here's why. It has occurred to me that the easiest way to see the point to everything we do is to figure out what would be missing if we just suddenly went away. When CF went away, did products stop making it to store shelves? No! Millions of tons of freight simply crossed the country on trucks with a different logo, each of which instantly got a little bigger and a little richer. What about the CF profits? Well they went away years earlier so they won't really be missed. The transition was virtually unnoticed. Did Wall Street go reeling, sending our economy into a tailspin? Hardly. In fact, it almost vanished without a trace with one small exception. Thousands of individual people who gave their hearts and their souls to CF lost their livelihoods, their retirement security, and their dreams of the future. Plans to buy the retirement home, send kids to college, and visit family and friends on vacations were swept away literally overnight. Worse yet, so many who considered themselves not just a person but part of the CF family, lost family members—people they may never see or talk to again. They lost not only their jobs, but also their identities. Many may never fully recover. In retrospect it's the only thing I can find that is missing in the wake of CF's demise. In the final paradoxical analysis, it's the only reason CF existed. It's the only reason that any company exists. CF, like all companies, existed for the people it served. It existed not to improve the standard of living, but to improve the quality of life for those lives that it touched.

Here in the western world we take for granted the robust economy and the quality of life it affords. That quality of life depends on the success of the individuals and the companies that drive the economy. The success of each company depends on the combined successes of the individual people that fill positions within the company. People drive the company's success, and the company, in turn, drives success for individual people within the company. Then, at the macro level, each company plays a part in driving the economy, which in turn drives demand for each company's offering. The strong economy thereby improves the quality of life enjoyed by the people living within that economy.

Still not convinced? Consider that CF and Freightliner were created during the Great Depression. When you employ people, you create wealth. Wealth begets consumers who buy goods from companies that employ people. Again, if you want learn why something exists, examine what would be missing if it went away. Today millions of people around the world live in abject poverty. Their quality of life suffers due to a poor economy. Robust commerce from effective companies made up of people improves the quality of life for people within and outside of every company.

If you take a real close look, a company is not a thing in and of itself; it's a concept, a series of legal documents, a person or group of people, and an idea. People don't exist for their companies; companies exist for people. With that in mind, again ask yourself the question I posed at the beginning of this chapter, "What is the purpose of a company?" If your answer was somewhere along the lines of, "To improve the quality of the lives of the people we touch by providing a, b, c…" you get it.

Who are those people?

Strong companies touch so many lives. Most obvious are those people who receive paychecks from the company. That, however, is not the beginning and the end of the list. The people operating within those companies touch so many other lives. Most of the lives they touch are of people they will never meet. Lives that will be touched (in a good or a bad way) include what I refer to as *The Big 10*.

1. Employees.
2. The friends and families of employees.
3. Customers.
4. The friends and families of customers.
5. Suppliers.
6. The friends and families of suppliers.

7. The people within the community in which it operates. Depending on the scope of the organization, it may impact communities around the world.
8. The friends and family of the people within the community.
9. Owners/Investors.
10. The friends and families of owners/investors.

If you are not somehow positively impacting one of these ten categories each day, you have wasted that day. Worse yet, if you're not careful, you may be negatively affecting some or all of those ten categories and not even know it!

At this point, it's worth taking a closer look at categories 9 and 10 because they seem to be the most misunderstood. Far too many employees spend the bulk of their professional activity attempting to satisfy the owners/investors by focusing exclusively on profits. Typically, this is not because it's the right thing to do, but because the owners have the ability to cut them loose and destroy their quality of life. At worst, employees not only focus exclusively on profits but on short-term profits. This is especially prevalent in publicly traded companies driving quarterly results. This culture can create a great deal of bitterness and confusion for employees who seek to satisfy the other eight categories, but aren't given the opportunity to do so. You know this is happening when you hear comments like, "All they care about is profit, not people; what's the point?"

Before I get misquoted and labeled a bleeding heart, the role of profit must also be defined. It's critical to every mission. First, we need to lose the image of the overbearing, overweight, cigar-smoking ogre in the ivory tower scamming his customers and abusing his employees out of greed. In publicly traded companies, the *owners* are anyone who buys shares of the company. In many cases, the largest group of investors is the variety of mutual funds being held in 401(k) plans with money from thousands of individual working people looking toward retirement. By satisfying owners in these cases, you're actually contributing to the quality of life of many other categories within the Big 10.

In a more simplistic tone, profits are the lifeblood of any business. Without profits, nothing happens. Suppliers don't get paid, employees don't get checks, and eventually the community loses jobs. Profits drive growth and innovation. CF could never have accomplished what it did without a robust stream of income to fund the research, building, and growth. It only went out of business when it failed to produce the necessary profit on a consistent basis.

Good business is separated from bad business by its ability to positively impact many of the categories without negatively impacting others. Driving any one or two without regard for *all* of the others is suicide. The key then is balance, and it's anything but easy.

What does any of this have to do with selling? It has everything to do with selling. When you go to the store to buy food for dinner, someone sold the produce to the store. Once it was sold to the store, it was delivered, probably on a truck. Someone sold the truck to that trucking company which hired someone to convince the produce company to use it to ship to your local supermarket. If you had a medical emergency, you might call 911. When you did, you used a phone that someone sold to you, and the ambulance that arrives shows up on tires that someone sold to them. Making sure the ambulance doesn't break down on the way might depend on someone selling the right oil to keep the engine running dependably. When you reach the hospital, someone sold the hospital *all* of the equipment used to treat your illness. When it's dangerously cold, we heat our homes with furnaces that someone sold to us. And it goes on and on ad infinitum.

The quality of life that we all enjoy is inextricably linked to the economy. The robust economy depends entirely on the effectiveness of the sales effort that keeps it moving. If you think that your only responsibility is to make a sale and generate a profit, you're being irresponsible.

Few activities are as critical to the quality of life that we enjoy as the professional sales effort. It's an awesome responsibility. Yet so many salespeople are embarrassed and ashamed to admit that they are salespeople. They tell you that they are "in the medical profession" when they sell pharmaceuticals or they're "Territory Managers" when they sell tires.

How and why does this happen? Because, for the most part, we've been doing it wrong for so many years and succeeding by accident. The few sales superstars that I've met are the few who, for whatever reason, understand and embrace the balance and the awesome responsibility. For these top achievers, selling is not something that is done *to* their customers; it's something that's done *for* them.

As you read this book, please keep one thing in mind. *Success* is measured in terms of your quality of life, not merely your standard of living. Quality of life involves people while standard of living is all about things.

Starting Fresh

"You must unlearn what you have learned"—*Yoda (Star Wars)*

In order for this book to be effective, you will need to abandon many of the skills and methods that helped you get to where you are now. It will be, at the very least, uncomfortable. It may be downright frightening. When we are brand new, we feel exposed and vulnerable. The training and experience we gain early in our career become walls that we use to build our houses, our lives. Mid-career training serves only to nudge the walls outward inch by inch. The longer the walls have been in place, the harder they will be to move. Eventually, each of us nudges the walls out until our career reaches its comfort zone. We're not soaring, but we're not struggling either. The inability to break down those walls and leave the self vulnerable is what keeps any salesperson from ever realizing his or her true potential. Furthermore, there is a line for each of us separating what we believe is possible from what we believe to be impossible. The only way to really find that line is to venture beyond it into that believed to be impossible. Just as Columbus sailed off into what most believed was the end of the earth, you too must have the courage to travel beyond conventional thinking. You must break down your walls!

Selling is more of an art form than a skill which is why it's so tough to teach and to learn. In *Selling By The Numbers,* I'm going to reduce the process into individual components that you can examine and understand. We'll talk about how to perform each one correctly. At first, it may seem stiff and regimented, and it won't look like much until it all starts to come together. After you've mustered up the patience, tenacity and discipline to complete the process, you can venture out and develop your own unique and powerful style. Only after you master the fundamentals will you be able to master the art form. This book is an outline for achieving the level of sales success that you desire and deserve whether you are building or rebuilding a career in commissioned outside sales.

Before we dive into exploring the right way, let's take a look at the many wrong ways that have led to frustration for so many salespeople. Here are five of the most popular and least effective methods taught to outside salespeople.

➤ So many methods, so little time!
➤ The curse of charisma
➤ Mastering the techniques
➤ The *JWH (Just Work Harder)* trap
➤ If you can't dazzle them with brilliance, baffle them with BS

Method 1: So Many Methods, So Little Time!

There seems to be an accepted notion that we each have to find our own style, and that one person's style will not work if forced upon another. Therefore many sales training programs, books, videos, and so forth tend to expose sales trainees to yet another novel approach, hoping they'll piece together one that works well for them. While this approach may eventually provide some level of success for most developing salespeople, it relies far too heavily on luck. It's essentially a trial-and-error approach that takes far too long. It becomes frustrating and demoralizing in the process, and it leaves an awful lot of bodies in its wake (salespeople as well customers)!

A rookie salesperson may start by practicing the first method that he or she is exposed to. If that method doesn't fit, he or she moves on to a different one. This practice of bouncing from method to method continues until the fateful day that he or she happens onto that perfect prospect. You know the one. It's the buyer who was completely loyal to his or her current supplier, but just had a disagreement. This prospect is ready to switch right now, and the rookie salesperson was the first one to walk in the door. Since it led to a sale on that day, the rookie will embrace that method for a while. Months, even years may go by before the rookie comes upon another perfect opportunity, yet he or she may continue using that method with increasing frustration. When the rookie finally figures out that it's not bearing fruit on a continual basis, it's off to the next method.

Without knowing precisely how to get the job done, you'll try each method hoping one will work. If the one you're trying feels promising, you'll pick up the pace with increased energy and enthusiasm. After wandering aimlessly through the abyss, you may begin to wonder whether or not you chose the right method. Gradually the enthusiasm fades while fear, uncertainty, and frustration set in. Finding real success in this manner becomes a matter of luck. I don't believe in luck. If you've felt this frustration and said to yourself, "There has got to be a better way," continue reading.

Method 2: The Curse of Charisma

Somewhere along your career path, you were told that there is such a thing as a "born salesperson." This is the man or woman who can get the meeting with that elusive prospect. This person seems to have all the right answers at just the right time and presents them in just the right way with confidence. This is the person who can "sell ice to an Eskimo" or "water to a drowning man." If you have ever felt like selling might not be for you since you weren't born with this "gift for gab," I urge you to reconsider. This trait is called charisma and it's both a blessing and a curse.

It's a blessing because charismatic people are, by definition, likeable. Conversation with them is fun, and people generally enjoy being around them. Charisma gets them in the door, but that's all. Once in the door, however, charisma alone won't get the job done. These so-called born salespeople tend to rely heavily on their charisma and can't figure out why their new friend won't say yes. Somewhere in the process, before the prospect will say yes, he begins to wonder, as the Wendy's commercials used to say, "Where's the beef!" Getting in the door is very easy for these charismatic people, so they rarely take the time to hone genuine selling skills. They become doomed to mediocrity and never reach champion status. Without exception, every champion I've met takes the selling profession very seriously. They believe that "good enough" rarely is. The best salespeople I know started out weak and were forced to learn how to do it the right way.

But wait, there's more! Charisma, overplayed, can actually work against you in a selling environment. Charismatic people are smooth talkers. I'm convinced that excessive charisma hurt Al Gore in his presidential debate with George Bush. Gore, a much more charismatic speaker, should have walked away with that debate. When it was over, many of the experts called Bush more credible. He wasn't nearly as polished, so he was considered to be more genuine. The more genuine people feel that you are, the more they will trust you. This has a profound impact in sales. We've all been talked into doing something that we later regret. When it happens, the offender is typically a smooth talker. It's not that we didn't put up any objections, the salesperson just had quick, reasonable answers to those objections, and they came naturally. Later, when buyer's remorse sets in, we feel foolish. We try to understand how we fell for it and vow we'll never let it happen again.

Here's how it happens. Consider the polygraph or lie detector machine. It's called a polygraph because the participant sits in a chair with a variety of electronic sensors that simultaneously graph physiological changes in heart rate, blood pressure, respiration, and perspiration. The polygraph session begins with a series of questions to which the answer is obviously right or wrong, such as "What is your name?" then moves into the core of the tough questions. The theory is that if the participant is lying, he or she will display subtle physiological changes. The lie detector obviously cannot compare verbal answers to facts, so it requires the machine's operator to interpret the participant's reaction to the questions and assess the likelihood that the response is a lie. In reality, the polygraph does *not* show whether or not a person is lying, only whether or not the participant is comfortable with his or her response. It's difficult to tell whether a participant is lying or is simply very uncomfortable answering the question. Likewise, it's difficult to distinguish between the truth and a lie if the participant is completely comfortable and at ease when telling a lie.

Each of us has a built-in polygraph machine or lie detector. In a focused one-on-one interview, each of us is will identify these same changes in the person with whom we're speaking. We, either consciously or subconsciously, sense physiological changes including eye movement, breathing, facial expression, and body language. Perhaps even more telling is timing. When under pressure, people tend to speak more quickly. When unsure, people tend to pause between words.

Like a polygraph, our internal lie detectors are not foolproof. When approached by a charismatic person, the subconscious mind sets off an alarm. It is, in effect, telling us that this salesperson is capable of deceiving me since I am not receiving any negative signals. Charismatic people can stay relaxed, cool, and undaunted in the face of severe pressure.

While typically viewed as a positive trait, charisma can be a curse for a salesperson. Highly charismatic people can completely suppress signals of discomfort or uneasiness, which is why they're so smooth. When they do this, they disable their prospect's internal lie detector, increasing the amount of time needed to establish real trust. Furthermore, if their prospect has a problem, they may be under a lot of pressure to find solutions. Charismatic people stay cool under pressure and may inadvertently appear not to take their prospect's problem seriously. If the prospect can't get a good "feel" for where the salesperson is coming from, there is no trust. If there is no trust, there is no sale.

How your prospects will deal with this questionable trust depends on several factors:

➤ Are their decisions based more on emotions or logic?
➤ How trusting are they by nature?
➤ Do they view themselves as too trusting?
➤ Do they trust their own judgment and intuition?
➤ Have they been burned before, and how badly?
➤ How perceptive are they?
➤ How perceptive do they feel they are?
➤ How large a risk are you attempting to get them to take?

Don't confuse charisma with confidence. Charisma means you can handle the situation. Confidence means you can handle problems. Charisma means *you're* likeable and comfortable. Confidence means your prospect is in good hands so *he* feels comfortable.

Confidence breeds trust, and trust drives sales. As you hone your craft, you will exude a type of confidence that goes beyond simple charisma. Confidence comes from knowing what you're doing and knowing how to do it. Confident people take comfort in the knowledge that they can be effective in important situations. When you know that you fully understand your prospect's problems and you know from hands-on experience that you can solve those problems, your confidence will be contagious. If you are relying on charisma to overcome a lack of confidence, you're really just being a liar.

Selling by the numbers is a system that gives you confidence. It eliminates the need for charisma and diminishes any negative impact it may have.

Method 3: Mastering the Techniques

Some training methods present closing techniques such as the alternate of choice, the assumptive, the scarce supply, reduction to the ridiculous, and so many more. They're called *closing techniques* because they bring the sales process to a close. If you're selling to the masses and you have one shot at your prospect, these techniques might work. If that's the case, this book is probably not for you. Whether selling Business to Business (B2B) or selling to individuals, recurring sales are very different from one-shot selling. With recurring sales, you don't want to close the relationship, you want to open it. Salespeople who utilize these techniques tend to disregard the situation at hand while hurling one piece of artillery after another hoping that one will eventually do the trick. Make no mistake about it, techniques are tricks, and tricks don't improve lives. Tricks erode quality of life.

Here are some of the problems with techniques.

➤ You probably have some techniques that have been in your arsenal so long that you don't quite remember how to use them. If you inadvertently use them wrongly, the results can be disastrous.

➤ You may have amassed so many techniques that you forgot some of them altogether.

➤ There are some you might have tried once or twice and, since they didn't work, you stopped using them.

➤ The few that were effective, you now use exclusively. You use them so frequently that they're getting worn out.

➤ If a technique is moderately effective and easy to use, you can bet that many of your competitors have used or are using it too.

Before long, your prospect figures out what's happening. Once that occurs, your technique is rendered useless. Worse yet, if your prospect figures out that you're using tricks and techniques, he or she might take off before you have a chance for one of them to work. Prospects become afraid of you.

If you bought this book hoping for a half dozen or so new techniques that you haven't tried yet, I'm sorry to disappoint you. Sales champions don't use tricks or techniques, but they are aware of them so that they can let their prospects know when one is being used against them.

Method 4: The JWH (Just Work Harder) Trap

If you're making your numbers, no one cares how hard you're working.
If you're not making your numbers, no one cares how hard you're working.

It takes a different mindset to be successful in outside sales. If you've been trained to believe that sales success comes from working long hours and making a lot of sales calls, then you've been trained to focus on activity instead of productivity, and you've been done a great disservice. If a top producer can accomplish his or her sales objectives by working two hours per week, a sales manager should not want to reprimand him or her. The manager should want to learn from the top producer! If an underachiever is working long hours making tons of calls and can't land a new customer, that person is of little use to the organization. Having been in sales and in sales management for over 20 years, I've met sales superstars who work 20 to 30 hours per week and continuously surpass their objectives. I've met struggling salespeople who work 60 to 70 hours per week who can't make even minimal, break-even objectives.

Far too many believe that success or failure in selling is just a matter of how hard you're willing to work. It was so early in my sales career that I can't even remember the first time I heard that theory. I still hear it more frequently today than any other selling advice, and it could not be more wrong. This antiquated formula for success in selling goes something like this: If you want to make more money, you simply have to work harder. There is a sea of prospects out there, and if you can get in front of enough of them, you will eventually earn their business. As an example, if you have 50 customers now and earn $50,000 in commission from those customers, in order to earn $100,000 in commissions, you need 100 customers, 50 more than you have now. The system goes on to explain that, theoretically, if it takes six calls to land a customer, you need to make at least 300 sales calls (50 new customers, six calls each). Wow, see how easy it is? Sales managers who buy into this formula believe that any salesman who's not cutting it simply needs to *make more calls*. It's just a matter of being in front of enough prospects so that the precise moment that they get mad at their current supplier and want to switch, you'll be there. Put simply, these people believe that they're better off being lucky than good and the harder they work the luckier they'll be.

JWH works just barely well enough to have survived as a primary strategy all these years.

This activity is great early in a sales career, but for different reasons. When you're new, you need to meet all of the players and learn the landscape. We'll cover this in greater detail later in the book. But the approach eventually leads to frustration. Once you start building a client base, your free time becomes scarce. If you're working eight hours per day to make $50,000, you will theoretically need to work 16 hours per day to make $100,000! How exciting is that? How feasible is that? Is it even possible? Salespeople who buy into JWH as a primary method will eventually hit a glass ceiling. They work harder than ever and have no time left at the end of the day to add any more. They now see their earning potential as limited and become frustrated wondering, "Is this all that there is?" They find themselves having to choose between their standard of living and their quality of life. When their sales manager tells them that their earning potential is virtually unlimited, they don't buy it, and they shouldn't. Plus, making numerous calls with nothing new to talk about gets demoralizing. After a while, your prospect will become unavailable, disinterested or downright irritated. You will become a nuisance. The stakes are high and the demands are great. You won't be successful if you're demoralized and your prospects are irritated. You must get up every morning fired up and excited about your challenge.

Another problem with JWH is that it depends on luck. Depending upon luck is a bad strategy for life! Every day, thousands of commercial and private airplane flights take off and land without incident. Before the Wright brothers, however, hundreds had experimented and failed. Flying, it turns out, depends on a few simple natural laws. The shape of the wing when moving through the air creates a low pressure on top and a higher pressure on the bottom. The action of the low pressure sucking the wing upward and the higher pressure underneath pushing it upward creates the *lift* that causes a plane to fly. The faster it goes, the more lift that is created. Temperature and altitude also affect

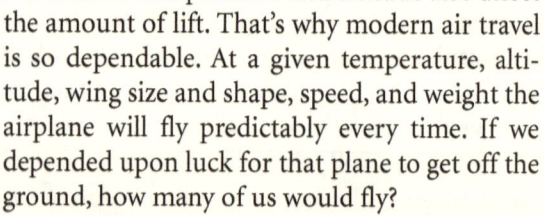
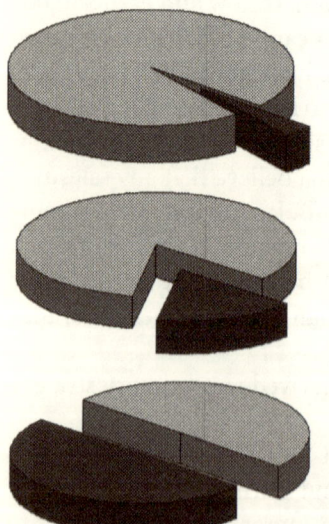

the amount of lift. That's why modern air travel is so dependable. At a given temperature, altitude, wing size and shape, speed, and weight the airplane will fly predictably every time. If we depended upon luck for that plane to get off the ground, how many of us would fly?

So when does JWH work? When does quantity of calls become more important than quality? If your company has done business with this account before and, for whatever reason, let them down, frequent consistent visits may be needed to reestablish credibility.

According to author and sales trainer Phil Wexler, for every customer that complains, 27 will have had a similar problem but didn't complain. Can you guess what the other 27 did instead? They went away and vowed never to return. It's also likely that they told most of their friends about it. You may be surprised one day to find that a tough prospect that just won't give you the time of day has written you off long before you met because he or she knows someone you let down years before.

Wexler goes on to say that for every six complainers (which means there were 156 non-complainers that just went away) five of the six will return even if you don't solve it to their satisfaction as long as the customer perceives the person who took the complaint to be friendly, enthusiastic, non-combative and, most importantly, *committed to the long-term nature of the relationship.*

In fact, three of the six complainers will probably not return even after you gave them what they want if you do it in a way that's cold, aloof, defensive, or if they sense you are *not committed to the long-term nature of the relationship.*

Consistent repeated calls on this type of prospect are very different from trying to wear them down in a JWH sales approach. You, as their potential future representative, must establish beyond any doubt that you are not like your predecessor. Most importantly, you must prove that you are totally committed to the long-term nature of the relationship. There are no shortcuts, and a hard-sell approach would be fatal. The only real way for the prospect to see if you'll have staying power when the going gets tough is for the prospect to make it tough and see if you keep coming back.

At the core of JWH is an implication that all prospects will eventually be unhappy with their current supplier at some point in time and you just need to be there and ready when it happens. It's like marketing a refrigerator. You'll run lots of ads every week so that the minute your prospect's fridge croaks, they'll buy from you. But there are two problems. First, staying in front of that many people waiting for an opportunity is time consuming and expensive. Secondly, when they are ready to switch, they'll probably explore your competition before making the switch. Third, and I've seen it happen more times than I can count, if you get busy and miss them on that fateful day, you'll lose the sale, and you will have wasted all that time!

If JWH is a bad method, why do so many managers use it? Because it's easy! Making joint calls, trouble-shooting call effectiveness, training time management, honing communication skills, and increasing product and industry knowledge all take time, skill, energy, effort, enthusiasm, experience, expertise, and patience. These are traits that sales managers may not have. Even if they do have those attributes, they simply may not have the time or patience to use them. With JWH, a sales manager simply has to review a call report and demand more calls. It's an overly simplistic way to look at the selling profession, and it doesn't work long-term. Worse yet, if a company exists for the people it serves, this method does not improve the quality of life for salespeople or customers; it just perpetuates mediocrity on a larger scale.

Method 5: If You Can't Dazzle Them with Brilliance, Baffle Them with BS

Some salespeople talk and talk about their product's features and benefits hoping that they'll hit a hot button. These salespeople tend to place far too much emphasis on product knowledge. Don't get me wrong, it is important to know your product. It's equally important to know your competitor's product so that you can compare and contrast. Product knowledge is worthwhile, but it's not enough. According to Tom Hopkins, world famous sales trainer, "People will say yes more on your conviction and enthusiasm than on your product knowledge." Furthermore, few things are so demonstratively superior that they can be labeled the very best in all circumstances. If they are, they will soon have no competitors. Each product may be uniquely effective in one specific application, but not in another. If you were selling shoes, would you say that a $400 Italian loafer is better than a $100 running shoe? I guess that depends on what you're planning to use it for. Using product knowledge to advance a sale requires knowledge of specific applications where your product or service excels and, more importantly, the discipline to get to know your prospect well enough to learn whether or not they want and need that benefit. A full-scale assault using features and benefits often blows past that second step. As you'll see, it's the most important step in the selling process. You improve lives by uncovering desires and matching your product or service to those desires.

"Don't worry, Mr. Prospect. If I don't know the answer to your question, I'll make something up."

Some salespeople strive for complete product knowledge because they're afraid to say, "I don't know." This is because they don't understand the power of those three simple words. When you say, "I don't know, but I'll find out" you invite your prospect to schedule a follow-up meeting. You have a chance to find documentation supporting whatever you say and have time to consider how the additional information will impact the decision. You also get a chance to hone in on key decision criteria. You might say, "I don't know, but I'll find out; tell me why that's important to you." This reply works so much better than a quick answer to the question. In its simplest form, "I don't know" disarms your prospect. It's honest and sincere and can be used to ask for a foot in the door. If you're asked, "Why is your product better than the one I'm currently using," turn the tables. Try saying something like, "I'd like us to learn together whether or not my product or service can help *your specific application*. If it does, it's good for both of us. If it doesn't, we'll both learn something. Since your time is valuable and so is mine, I wouldn't suggest this approach unless I was confident that it has a real chance of working. Is there somewhere in your business we can test against the competition?"

Whenever possible, don't rely on lip service. Any argument will be more convincing when you put your money where your mouth is. For example "If it works, I'll save you money, time, aggravation, whatever. If it doesn't, I'll give you back the difference." If you're really sure, sweeten the pot by saying something like "Mr. Prospect, I'm so certain that we'll save you money that, if I can't, I'll give you back the difference and I'll take you out for a steak dinner!" As a salesperson, this is a win-win. Agreement to going out for dinner is an advance where you will have a chance to bond with your new customer. Hope is our salvation. No matter how good their existing supplier is, your prospect will always wonder if it could be better.

Selling is a tremendous profession if you are successful. If you're not successful, the job sucks. That's what *Selling by the Numbers* is all about. Instead of filling a book with a hundred selling ideas that might make you successful, I've outlined a systematic sales process that any salesperson can use to realize success and virtually eliminate any chance of failure. More importantly, the system is designed to keep all of your life goals in the equation helping you to achieve balance and improve overall quality of life.

Selling is not a game. Selling is the essence of the American dream. The high standard of living we enjoy depends upon a robust economy. In order for an organization to provide its employees with a high standard of living, it must stay competitive. It must be aware of and have access to anything and everything that's available to make it stronger. If those products and services exist, but no one knows about them, they cannot help. Your job as a salesperson is to help as many people as possible become aware of your products and services and to help them determine how they might use your products or services to enrich their lives and the lives of others.

Before you read on, find a quiet place without distractions and ask yourself this one crucial question. Do you really, honestly, from the bottom of your heart and soul believe in the product or service you are selling? Does it solve a problem? Does it make life better, easier, safer, more fun, or more secure for someone? Would someone in the world be a little bit worse off if you weren't there to provide this product or service? If the answer is yes, you're heading the right direction. If the answer is no, you will become increasingly demoralized trying to sell it. To be successful, selling must be something that you do for your customers, and not something that you do to them.

2

Motivation

"In the power to change yourself is the power to change the world around you."
—Anwar Sadat

Motivating Change
You can lead a horse to water, but you cannot make it drink.

The principles of motivation impact everything you do every day. That's why motivation is the very first concept you must grasp and grasp fully. Selling by the numbers is all about change. You must change how you view and approach your career as you learn how to change what your prospects choose to buy. Change is about motivation. Whether I'm asking you to buy-in to my selling system or I'm asking someone to buy a product, I will need to motivate a change. Motivation is about choices. Even when you choose not to decide, you've still made a choice.

You can encourage, inspire, influence, convince, or persuade, but you cannot force anyone to do anything. You probably think that you could force someone to act if you had enough power, the proverbial "gun to the head." Actually, that's just a form of motivation, a choice. If a criminal approaches you with a gun and demands that you give him your money, you must choose between giving it to him or getting shot. The criminal hopes that you will consider only those two options, and quickly decide on option one. When the criminal presents the gun, he is in essence offering the most compelling argument he is capable of providing, but he, too, is taking a risk. He might be overpowered and have his "argument" (the gun) used against him. He may be apprehended by the authorities and go to prison. You may call his bluff, try talking him out of it or you might flee. You may wonder if, even after giving him your money, he'll shoot anyway.

Your decision, while taking place in a fraction of a second will depend on many factors including but not limited to the location, how much money you have to protect, your physical stature compared to his, your proximity to your assailant, the weather, the lighting, previous experience in similar situations and so much more. You are at a significant disadvantage since the criminal is likely to have chosen you, the time, and the place because they seemed to be in his favor. What he can't be sure of is how you will choose to respond. If your choice is to draw your own gun, the decision then becomes his to make.

The very best illustration of this is a scene from a Clint Eastwood movie. It's one of the classic scenes in contemporary movie history. Near the end of a grueling foot pursuit and shoot-out, detective Harry Callahan, played by Clint Eastwood, has his suspect cornered when he says "I know what you're thinking, punk. You're thinking, 'Did he fire six shots or only five?' To tell you the truth, in all this excitement, I've kinda loss track myself. But being this is a .44

Magnum, the most powerful handgun in the world, able to blow your head clean off, you have to ask yourself a question. 'Do I feel lucky?' Well do ya' punk?" The detective was offering a choice. If you saw the movie, you'd know the criminal made the wrong decision! Detective Callahan could not *make* him surrender. He could only offer him a choice.

Helping People Get What They Want.

"You can get everything you want in life if you will just help enough other people get what they want."—Zig Ziglar

To understand motivation, think in terms of motive. Motive is a reason to change, a reason for doing something different. A sale, in its purest form is the result of your prospect's motivation to change. When you're selling, you're working to improve your customer's life. You may do this by motivating them to do something, or encouraging a behavior (buy from you). Or you may do it by motivating them to stop doing something, or discouraging a behavior (stop buying from your competitor). It's just different ways of saying the same thing. One of the best books I've read about motivation is entitled *Bringing out the Best in People* by Aubrey C. Daniels. If you want to dig deeply into factors influencing motivation, check it out.

In order for your prospect to become motivated to do something, he or she must be convinced that their life will improve because they will get something that they want or avoid something that they don't want. In order to stop doing something, he or she must be convinced that, if they continue, their quality of life will diminish because they will get something that they don't want or they will lose something that they want. It is that simple. These four factors are all that matter. You must be keenly aware of them throughout the sales solicitation process. Anything outside of them is chatter. The final decision to buy or not to buy will always come down to these four factors.

To encourage behavior:
- ✓ Give them something that they want.
- ✓ Help them lose something that they don't want.

To discourage behavior:
- ✓ Give them something that they don't want.
- ✓ Cause them to lose something that they want.

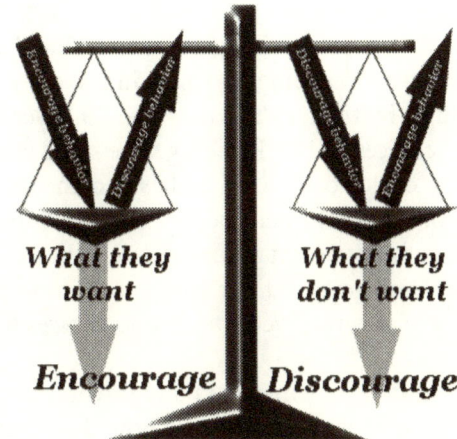

The essence of buying is a basic two-step process. Determine what your prospect wants and then figure out how to help them to get it, or determine what they don't want and figure out how to help them to avoid it. Only after clearly stating what is wanted does the buying process begin. If our prospects won't tell us what they want, we can't motivate them to buy; end of story. It's simple, but simple doesn't mean easy.

Getting People to Tell You What They Want
"Tell me what you want, what you really, really want"—The Spice Girls

It would be so easy if our prospects would just tell us what they want. Then all we would have to do is to show them how we can help them to get it. But often, they won't. If they really want something, why won't they just come out and tell us what it is? Here are the 13 biggest reasons.

1. Getting what you want is the easy part. Deciding what you want—that's the tough part.

Our prospects today are faced with so many choices. Choosing any single one usually means there are several that they will have to do without. In addition, if there is a monetary cost involved with what they want, they will also have to evaluate it against all the other things they might buy with the money, then figure out which will have the greatest impact on their overall quality of life.

More than at any time in history, the choices today are staggering, even paralyzing. If you don't believe me, think about the last time you asked, "What would you like to eat for dinner?" This, I suspect, is a discussion that rarely took place during the Stone Age. If it ran past the cave, it was dinner.

There's a great book written by Jack Trout entitled *Differentiate or Die*. In this book is a terrific chart illustrating the explosion in the number of choices we face. According to Trout, in the early '70s Frito-Lay offered 10 varieties of chips. By the late '90s they had 78. Over the counter pain relievers went from 17 choices to 141. Running shoe styles went from 5 to 285, and the list goes on. The explosion in choices has become so daunting that an entire industry has evolved just to help people choose. Publications like Consumer Reports and Zagat's restaurant guides supplement the literally millions of Web sites arming the average consumer with more information than they can possibly digest. There are even Web sites listing choices for which publications are available to help you choose.

Years ago, I managed a high volume, mass merchandising retail tire store. This company understood how daunting the decision process was and took full advantage of it. Since tires are all round and black, differentiating between them can be difficult. Buyers tend to fall into one of two categories. First is the dreaded price buyer who says, "They all look about the same so give me the cheapest one you've got." It's simple enough to close this sale if you have the cheapest product on the street. If you don't, you're sunk. The second buyer looks for top name brands at the lowest price. He or she says essentially, "I know there is some difference between the cheapest and the most expensive but I can't tell what it is so I'll stick with a recognized brand name that I trust." You can quickly close this sale if you have a brand that they trust *and* you have it at the lowest price in town. After all, your tire and your competitor's tire are the same brand and model so why pay more? At the tire store I managed, full-page newspaper ads would draw them in. Highlighted in the ad was the tag line "Top name brands at guaranteed lowest prices." Then, armed with the ad, the customers came in thinking that they knew what they wanted. Once they arrived at this tire store, however, they faced a dozen or more different tires for their application. To display them, we put one of each of the over 100 tire models in stands, side-by-side so that it looked like a long black tube of tires. To the consumer, while they all looked pretty similar, the range in price was dramatic. Once facing the tremendous selection, many became confused. And confused was just how this company wanted them to be. In order to get the customers in the door, this company marked these top brands up very little and the profit margins were razor thin. The goal for the salesperson was to move the expensive brand-name buyer down to the house brand in the middle by convincing him or her that they could get comparable quality at a lower price. "Why pay for the name?" This has been coined "selling up by selling down." What the brand conscious consumer did not know is that for $85 they were getting a name-brand tire that might cost the store $84, a $1 profit. While the $75 private brand alternative may save the consumer $40 on a set of four, the tire might come into the store at a cost of $50 allowing a much more robust profit. When facing the low-end buyer, the objective was to ease them up toward the middle by implying that personal safety may not be the best place to get stingy. On the low end, the $40 economy product might cost the store $39 also allowing the same measly $1 profit. The *safer* $60 tire that the salesman recommends might cost the store $45 again allowing a more substantial profit.

This tire store chain certainly did not invent this technique. It's been around a long time. Sales trainers call this the alternate of choice close. The alternate of choice close is an attempt to take your prospect out of his or her misery by distilling the many choices down to two or three suggestions and implies that your prospect will appreciate the gentle nudge. The two or three suggested are, of course, the ones *you* want to sell and not necessarily the ones that best suit the customer's needs. The next time you go to any large appliance store, clothing store or supermarket, look to see if you can find signs of this approach.

If you're still selling using this method, you've probably figured out that it doesn't work like it used to. That's a problem with techniques. If they work, everyone jumps on the bandwagon and starts to use them. Before long, the consumer faces it so frequently that they figure out what's happening. Once they do, two bad things happen. First, the technique stops working, and second, the mere attempt to use it immediately alienates your prospect because they feel they're being manipulated and that you can't be trusted.

Selling today is very different. We no longer live in the industrial age; we live in the information age. Consumers are savvier than at any time in history! The volume of information available to consumers is overwhelming. Unlike in the past, consumers know that, if they don't like the answers they're given, they can zip home and surf the Web to check accuracy.

Dealing with it—

Effective immediately, stop focusing on what you want as a salesperson and focus on your prospect. Go into every selling situation determined to help them navigate the myriad of options. Intimate working knowledge of your product or service is not enough. You must know your competitor's offering as well as your own. Instead of a stereotypical salesperson, you will be seen as a valuable resource. Then, and only then, will your prospects begin to tell you what they want since they now see you as someone who might help them to get it. With so many choices available, your customers need guidance more than ever. If you lose the tricks and techniques, your prospect will view you as a knowledgeable resource, and they'll hope to take advantage of your expertise and buy from you.

2. "We're not worthy."—Wayne and Garth

Picture yourself stopping into a dentist's office with a sore tooth. A person comes through a door wearing greasy torn jeans holding a hammer and a pair of pliers asking, "Who's next?" How likely are you to tell him what you want? Your prospects are deciding whether or not they want to do business with you from the moment they see you walk through the door, hear you call on the phone, or read your letter. And you can't ever be certain what their biases are. Your prospect may think that you're too young or that you're too old. He or she may find you to be too assertive or not assertive enough. He or she may think that you're overdressed, or that you're underdressed. The list goes on ad infinitum.

Dealing with it—

If you want your prospects to tell you what they want, they must feel comfortable dealing with you. You must prove yourself worthy from the very first contact. While many factors (height, age, gender, etc.) are obviously well beyond your control, it is important, that you examine everything that is within your control and strive to keep them as positive or neutral as possible. Prospects want to do business with people that they trust. The more your prospects feel you are like them, the more comfortable they will feel and the more they will trust you.

Don't rush! Trust is a tricky thing. It can take years to create and seconds to destroy. If you are asking your prospect to take a large risk, you should expect it to take more time to earn a sufficient amount of trust. If you rush it, you will erode the trust making the sales process take even longer. When asked a tough question, many salespeople feel compelled to answer the question quickly hoping to be viewed as an expert. They are afraid that, if they took some time to think about it, the prospect might think they're inexperienced and unworthy. In fact, the opposite is true. Tough questions, particularly technical questions, are best answered with written objective evidence. Prior to presenting the evidence, it is imperative that you ask a lot of questions to clarify the concern. This is counterintuitive for many salespeople, and it's a key differentiator between the very best and the mediocre. Quick cavalier answers do not demonstrate salesperson competence. They indicate impatience.

A better way to prove that you're a worthy resource is to respond to each question with clarifying questions until the concern is nailed down tight. Writing down the responses shows you care. Once crystal clear, tell your prospect that you know of various sources for data addressing those concerns and ask for a follow-up meeting so that you can bring the data in for his or her review. This approach offers so many benefits.

➤ Your prospect rarely comes across salespeople who will go the extra mile to sort through the sea of data to support their position. The effort has its own value.

➤ People believe what they see so much more than what they hear. Asking someone to take your word for it is a lot to ask, particularly when you are a salesperson, because in commission sales you're only paid if they get the answer that they want to hear.

➤ The time between the initial call and the follow-up gives you an opportunity to reflect upon the meeting. We've all heard that hind-sight is 20/20. How many times have you left a conversation only for it to dawn on you days later what you should have said?

➤ It gives you an opportunity to move past the first few concerns and dig deeper into the situation at hand. Once you clarify a concern and promise to research it, you can ask "What else should I be prepared to discuss that might impact the decision?" You'll learn that the first few concerns are generally presented just to see if you're even worth talk-ing to. Many salespeople give quick answers, then wonder why the process doesn't move closer to a sale. It's because you're still at the sur-face. To dig deeper, answer the question with a comment like, "That's a great question. I think I know where I can get some great information about that. So that I can be sure to thoroughly address your concern, tell me why it's important to you."

➤ Having an answer at hand for every question tends to display an "I've seen it all before" attitude. Each prospect is unique and wants to be treated as such.

➤ Perhaps most importantly, each additional visit increases trust. You establish a track record. Trust isn't about what you might do right here and now. Trust is about what you might do down the road when they really need you. Each separate occasion that your prospect witnesses you showing up promptly, dressing professionally, behaving consis-tently, and being prepared indicates that this is the way you really are and that they didn't just catch you on a good day.

3. Your Miranda Rights
You have the right to remain silent. Anything you say can and will be used against you.

We know that we need to ask questions if we want to reveal the desire and identify the opportunity. Effective questioning is the cornerstone to sales suc-cess. Many salespeople are reluctant to ask a lot of questions or to ask tough questions for fear of being considered pushy or confrontational. They are afraid of the interview becoming an interrogation, and they should be. Once it does, they have destroyed any hopes of uncovering desires. It's as if they need to read the prospect his or her Miranda rights prior to the questioning. This is the most prevalent reason that prospects won't just tell us what they want. They're afraid to!

What is the difference between questioning and interrogation?

If you come across as pushy or manipulative, your prospect will not answer any of your questions, at least not honestly. It's like "lawyering up." If they won't answer your questions, you stop moving forward in the selling process. The difference between questioning and interrogation lies not in the questions; it lies in the motive behind the questions. When a doctor asks a battery of questions, he or she is doing so in an effort to uncover the information needed to help you with a problem. When a detective interrogates with a battery of questions, he or she is doing so in an effort to uncover the information needed to bring you up on charges! You must focus on what your prospect is trying to achieve, not what you are trying to achieve. If your doctor asks "Where does it hurt?" and you answer by saying "It's none of your business!" your doctor is likely to say, "Look, do you want me to help or don't you?" When a detective asks "Where were you last Thursday evening?" and you respond with "It's none of your business!" it's usually because the detective is trying to nail you, not help you.

It's what I call cumulative case reasoning, a term I picked up from watching too many court TV shows, and it strikes fear in the hearts of many buyers. It goes something like this.

Detective: "Were you in that building?"
Suspect: "Yes, but not in that room."
Detective: "Do you own a knife?"
Suspect: "Yes, but I only use it for hunting."
Detective: "Did you argue with this person?"
Suspect: "Yes, but…"

And the sparring goes on and on. At the end of the interrogation, the detective simply says "Boy, you've got an excuse for everything, don't you?" The detective has proved nothing except that the suspect was sharp enough to overcome each question. It leaves a feeling, however, that there are far too many coincidences. In a selling interview, it goes something like this.

Salesperson: "Is this what you're looking for?"
Prospect: "Not really."
Salesperson: "Why not?"
Prospect: "I'm not crazy about the color."
Salesperson: "What color do you prefer?"
Prospect: "I guess I like red."
Salesperson: "Would you like me to see if I have one in red?"
Prospect: "Actually it's a little big too."
Salesperson: "I have a smaller model Would you like to see it?"
Prospect: "Perhaps, how much is that one?"
Salesperson: "About ten percent less, would you like one if I have it in red?

These scenarios may go on and on, or they may come to an abrupt halt. What's consistent in both is an attempt to achieve a selfish motive with little or no regard for the participant. The detective and the salesperson are trying to nail the other person as quickly as possible so that they can move on to the next one.

Dealing with It—

Many salespeople I've worked with over the years are surprised when they see how much information I can get a prospect to tell me. I have no secrets, I simply walk into each selling situation with a true desire to help that prospect determine what he or she wants and to figure out if there is any way I can help them to get it. Making the sale is not yet even a consideration. I'm continually asking, "How can I make them better, more effective, more productive, happier or more successful?" If I can help, I will. If I cannot help them, we'll part friends. Even if I can't help them right here and now, I may come across a product or service someday that can help. When I do, you can be certain that I'll stop by with it. If your motives are pure, doors will open. When you switch the focus off of what your prospect wants and onto what you want, your entire demeanor changes and doors start closing. If you're blatant, the doors don't just close, they lock! When your prospect can feel a genuine interest in his or her desires, they'll open up and tell you all you need to know to make the sale. Conversely, if you hit the streets each morning and say "Okay, who's my next victim?" your message will come through loud and clear, and your prospects will exercise their right to remain silent. If you want to open doors, remember this. Selling is not something that you do *to* your customers, it's something that you do *for* them.

4. How can you tell when a salesperson is lying?
"(His lips are moving!)"

Be aware that on most initial calls, you won't get to start at zero you start below zero. Your predecessors have long since set your prospect's expectations. Inept salespeople have made selling tougher and less lucrative for the rest of us. This was one of my first motivations for writing this book. I was hoping to reduce the number of terrible salespeople out there who are making the job so tough for those of us who do it right. Far too many ask just enough questions to pry open the door only to tell the prospect what they want to hear. If they can't quickly pry it open, they move on to the next. If you stop into a prospect following three or four of these predatory salespeople, what do you think the odds are of getting him or her to open up to you right away? Those of us determined to build long-term business relationships have to spend much more time convincing them that we're not like the others.

Dealing with It—
Of course, to convince your prospects that you're different, you must actually be different. Remember this, "Right is right even if no one is doing it, wrong is wrong even if everyone is doing it." Commit to the long-term nature of the relationship. If you can provide any testimonials from others who already do business with you, they'll help.

5. "Did you ever wonder if this is as good as it gets?"
—Jack Nicholson

We live in turbulent times. The dream of a great big beautiful tomorrow shining at the end of every day is clouded and many of us have a new perspective on life particularly since 9/11. A soft economy, corporate downsizing, rightsizing, layoffs, and bankruptcies have exacerbated the problem. While most still hope tomorrow will be better, many no longer take for granted what they currently have and will be content if they can just keep from moving backward. This is an awfully tough obstacles known colloquially as "If it ain't broke, don't fix it!" In engineering, it's called inertia. Calling on a prospect stuck in inertia is one of the toughest prospects you'll face. Inertia doesn't mean that they don't have problems. There are always problems, even if they're minor and insignificant. It simply means that they have no immediate crises. But the world does not stand still. Our environment continues to move forward with or without us. It has been said that, if you're standing still in a world that's moving forward, you are actually going backward. And, as I said earlier, when you decide to do nothing, you have still made a choice.

If a customer has a problem, even if it's a problem with you, you have something to talk about, work through, and learn from. Again, picture the dentist's office I mentioned earlier. If you have a sore tooth, you will at least talk to a dentist. If, as far as you know, everything is great, you won't even go to the dentist's office. For many, a minor cavity is not enough of a reason to take action. Once the pain gets serious, it's time for an office visit. Even though we all know that we're better off catching it early, minor problems don't get prioritized.

With inertia, dialogue stops fast and you have nothing to work with. Open ongoing dialogue is the network of roads we use to get from where we are to where we want to be in the selling process. When you come across a prospect stuck in inertia, it's as if there really isn't anything at all that they want or need that they don't have. How can you get someone to tell you what he or she wants if they act as if they don't want anything? *How can they not want anything?* Just because you or I want something, doesn't mean that everyone else does. That sounds obvious if we're talking material things such as our favorite foods, vacation destination, brand of automobile, etc. It's not so apparent when we're talking about elusive concepts such as success and happiness. Success and happiness are among the most vague, ambiguous, and variable words used in modern speech. We might assume that we all want to make more money, we all want to be physically fit, we all want to be free, etc. Not so. Many of your prospect's desires will be suppressed. Each time your prospect's hopes and dreams got revealed and squashed they became more reluctant to voice them again. This can be powerful stuff! If the hopes and dreams are strong and have been pent up for a long time, you may actually bring up anger and venom that was meant for a previous salesperson who let them down. Like a tank containing extreme pressure, you want to release the pressure slowly and systematically; otherwise you may witness an explosion that your selling process will not survive.

Dealing with It—

Progress within this scenario will be slow by design. Do not attempt to manipulate and push, or doors will shut in your face faster than you can ask, "Is it something I said?" Chill out! If this prospect is worthwhile, commit to the long-term nature of the process. You will need to thoroughly convince your prospect that you have their best interests at heart. Make sure to consider your questions carefully before you ask them. If you're asking a question that's in your best interest, reconsider. Only by asking questions regarding how you can best serve their best interests will you make progress.

6. Don't Kill My Future to Spare My Feelings

Fully 99 percent of the business people I've dealt with over the years are genuinely nice people, and most prospects really don't enjoy hurting your feelings. When you ask them how you might help, their responses are often shallow, giving you nothing to work with. There may be some deep-seated resentment toward you, your company, or salespeople in general that just won't come out into the open for fear of confrontation. Unless your prospect is a real jerk, he or she will go to great lengths to avoid confrontation. Likewise, salespeople tend to avoid asking pointed questions that might draw an attack.

You may justify avoiding the question in an effort to keep the sales interview upbeat. Your prospect may think that they're doing you a favor by sparing your feelings. In reality, he or she is doing you a tremendous disservice by eroding your opportunity and your future.

Dealing with It—

For genuine success, you will need to become the Orkin man. While no one really wants to open up the walls and see all the termites (hidden objections), rest assured that leaving them undiscovered will eventually cause the house to come down. Questions like, "Have you tried us before and how did it go?" are golden opportunities for sales progress. Yet so many salespeople avoid them out of fear of the response. The truth might hurt, but you need to hear it.

7. We Don't Desire Something We've Never Heard Of

It's been said that the goal of advertising is to make us feel like we've wanted our whole life something that five minutes ago we didn't even know existed. Your prospect won't tell you that they want something if they have never heard of it. If you are fortunate enough to be selling a universally exciting product that was just introduced, your product will sell itself. Your goal then is just to demonstrate it to enough people. Many salespeople go through their entire career hoping to represent that wonderfully unique product. Before you get too excited about it, remember that a product that sells itself doesn't really need you to sell it!

Dealing with It—

Since decidedly few of us have an intrinsically innovative and universally exciting product to sell, most of us need to find that excitement somewhere deep within the one we are selling. Once you do, a casual mention is all that it takes to pique your prospect's interest. Be careful not to make it sound larger that life. Remember that sales integrity is suspect and that most people believe that if something sounds too good to be true, it probably is.

8. To Dream the Impossible Dream

Does desire ever come from learning that something you thought was impossible now appears to be possible? The initial tendency is to answer this question yes. For example, there was an exciting new car that you liked a lot until you learned that the monthly payment far exceeded your budget. You then see a TV commercial advertising zero percent financing, or special incentives available for a limited time that bring it within reach. All of a sudden, you want it again, or do you? The truth is, you never really stopped wanting it. You just suppressed your desire because you were convinced there was no way you could get it. If you can get a prospect to tell you that there is something that he or she wants after they have pretended to stop wanting it, you've hit the mother lode. You really don't want to do this unless you're confident that you can help them to get it. There's nothing easy about extracting these gems. And one of the worse things you can do is to get a prospect to say, "You mean you can do that?" only to have to say "No, not really!" How you handle it when you do expose those desires takes skill and finesse.

Dealing with It—
It starts with intuition and awareness. Any time in the selling process that you witness a spark of interest or excitement, make a note of it. If there is something that your prospect really wanted but gave up, there will be subtle signs. Once you believe you've found a hidden desire, try to think of someone else that you've dealt with that you helped realize a similar dream. It doesn't have to be exactly the same, but it should be something equally as ambitious or far-fetched. Share that experience with your prospect. Tell them how excited you were to be the one who helped to make it happen. Effective salespeople are constantly making the impossible possible. Abraham Maslow once said, "Every really new idea looks crazy at first."

9. "What the head makes cloudy, the heart makes very clear." —Don Henley (The SHOULDS)

Until you uncover prospect wants and needs, you won't sell a thing. More importantly, you must know whether you have just uncovered a want or a need. Once you accomplish this, the road to completing the sale will appear. If you don't, you won't sell a thing. Determining what is a want and what is a need is tougher than it seems. Even Webster's uses the word *need* in nearly half of the definitions of the word *want* and uses the word *want* in many of the definitions of the word *need*. Conventional wisdom tells us that a need is just a stronger version of a want. It's as if the words are almost interchangeable, but they are not. Consequently, it's no wonder so many salespeople have difficulty moving the sale forward. If you are a cigarette smoker, you might tell yourself that you *need* to quit. A few hours later, you find that you really *want* a smoke, so you light one up. If you're overweight, you might tell yourself that you really *need* to lose a few pounds. A few hours later, you find that you really *want* a snack, so you chow down.

Needs come from the head. They are defined logically and rationally. Most people can describe what they need in fairly simple and direct terms. Wants come from the heart. They are defined emotionally, with feelings and are much tougher to describe. Sometimes, they are wanted "just because."

The problem with wants is that they often seem childish. Make no mistake about it, they are. Children have no problem figuring out what they want. It's just as simple for them to tell you when they want it, Now! Growing up sucks. We don't stop wanting things; we just suppress the desires because, intellectually, we convince ourselves that we don't really need them. William Burroughs is quoted as saying, "What you want to do is eventually what you will do anyway. Sooner or later."

If there is something that you want and need and the cost is low, you'll do it. If there's something that you don't want and don't need, you probably won't do it regardless of price.

You can need something that you don't want (getting a tooth pulled) and you can want something that you don't need (one more donut). When facing this type of dilemma, the first deciding factor is usually the price. If you really need it, don't particularly want it, but the cost is very low, you'll probably do it. Likewise, if you really want it, don't particularly need it, and the cost is very low, you're also likely to do it.

We are all aware that society has a set of rules that dictate what we should and shouldn't want. Oh boy, if ever there was a sinister little motivation killer coiled up behind a rock, it's the word "should." It can become very difficult to distinguish between not wanting something and wanting it, but convincing ourselves that we shouldn't want it because someone, somewhere has told us it is wrong to want it. Don't give me that. You know what I mean. The problem is, many of these are deep-rooted in morals. When they're rooted that deeply, you can hack away all you want, but you won't kill them. You may not have the energy to dig way down to the roots just to determine why they feel that way. Thousands of psychiatrists earn billions of dollars helping people figure out the early programming that factors into these decisions. Talk about pain! Psychiatrists often refer to a breakthrough, and it comes with a total loss of composure. Think of oil drillers slowly grinding away deeper and deeper for days, weeks, even months until BAM! They hit, and the oil is flying everywhere!

The programming that our prospects have that affects their desires is rooted just as deeply. If you work to release it, be sure you can handle it once it comes out.

Dealing with it—
The objective always lies deep within the want or the desire. If you can get someone to at least admit that they want something, you simply need to provide the rationalization to justify the decision logically. Rationalization will be covered in detail later in the book.

10. I just don't like change.
—(The COULDS)

There is a myth that people categorically resist change and it's just not true. People do not resist change when they are absolutely convinced that the change is for the better. If I convince you that the selling techniques presented in this book will make you a lot more money with the same or fewer hours worked and less stress, completely enhancing your overall quality of life, would you resist it? Not likely. If you resist it, it's probably not because you are resistant to change, but rather because I haven't successfully convinced you that my method is better than the one you are now using.

Often, the older people get, the more they resist change. When we're young, we have dreams of this wonderful life that we're going to enjoy some day. As kids, we talk about growing up to become an astronaut, a doctor, a rock star, a movie star, or whatever. When we muster up all our energy and courage and make the significant life changes needed to pursue those dreams, we become vulnerable. If and when the dream fails, we are much less likely to take a chance again. We learn from our mistakes. Each time we take a risk and fall short, we have one more reason not to risk in the future.

This is why we become increasingly resistant to change. Each failure makes us more aware of what *could* go wrong. Once we have an awareness of what could go wrong, any time we think of something good that we want, we start to consider what we might get that we don't want or what we might lose that we already have: the price of "going for it." And everything has a price. We've heard it all before, we fell for it once, and we're not falling for it again. The only real difference between an optimist and a pessimist is statistics. When it comes right down to the decision, the optimist is considering a high probability of success and a low probability of failure. The pessimist is convinced of a high probability of failure.

Change is about choices, and choices can be maddening. People like having choices; they just don't like to choose. If you choose and choose wrong, it's your fault. Whether or not they admit it, most people would rather not have a choice so that if something bad happens, it's not their fault. It's serendipity. There are probably hundreds of things that your prospects want: a bigger home, a stronger body, a newer car, more savings, higher education, a lower golf handicap, etc. Figuring out that they want these things is easy until they consider what they'll have to give up in order to get it. Then they must decide which they want more, the thing they'll get or the thing they will have to give up.

Dealing with it—

When your prospect tells you, "I just don't like change," you should be hearing, "You have not convinced me beyond any shadow of a doubt that the change you propose is for the better." They see potential downsides that outweigh the benefits. In short, you still have some work to do. You will need to consider what *could* go wrong and bring it to light. Expose and explore it. Far too many salespeople try to sweep those negatives under the rug and hope they go away, but they never really do. You will need to revisit their wants. If the change you're proposing doesn't clearly provide them with something they really want and it has even a modest risk, they will be reluctant to change.

11. Being in the Right Place at the Wrong Time

There is a natural progression in what people want. If you're talking to someone who isn't sure whether or not he or she will be eating tomorrow, they probably won't be spending much time thinking about what color their favorite new car would be? Abraham Maslow has depicted this in what has become known as the hierarchy of needs. According to Maslow, our desires come in stages. First and foremost, we focus on simple survival. Until we have food and water, little else matters. Once our survival needs are met, we seek safety and shelter. Beyond safety and shelter, we seek social connections such as friends and companions.

As we progress toward the top of the pyramid, many of us strive to achieve esteem and personal accomplishment. At the pinnacle is what has been referred to as self-actualization. This is the point where we become all of which we are truly capable. Decidedly few of us ever reach this level. If we're ready to move to the next level and we're absolutely certain we wouldn't lose anything we already have, we would do it. End of story. But that's like saying, "Don't go near the water until you learn how to swim." It doesn't work that way. Growth involves risk. Risk involves choice. Achievement and esteem come only by risking safety and security. This is a big reason why our prospects won't tell us what they want. They can't ever be certain of what they're risking, and they can't be sure that it's worth what they might lose.

Dealing with It—

When you are exploring what might motivate your prospect, you need to aware of where they are in the pyramid. As stated earlier, motivation to change involves getting something they want (moving up the pyramid) or avoiding something that they don't want (moving down). Until you know where they are at this very moment, you can't know if the level you're suggesting is higher or lower than where they are now! Beyond that, you must be in tune with their comfort level regarding risk. More conservative prospects will require much more assurance and guarantee before they dip their toe in the water. Risk takers jump right in.

12. If I Told You, I'm Afraid I'd Have to Kill You

What are the odds of someone telling you what they really want if they feel that, armed with the knowledge, you might be in a position to hurt them?

Scenario 1, Large-Company Politics

When selling to a very large company, be aware that problems are not only tolerated, they're ignored, rationalized, overlooked, covered up, and kept secret. We've all been in front of the decision maker behind the mahogany desk who tells us that their current program works just fine. Down on the street, however, you may witness otherwise. That's because the people down in the trenches go to great lengths to keep any problems a secret. "What HQ doesn't know won't hurt them." This is especially true when HQ is the problem. Up in the ivory tower, top management wants to hear that their bold new programs are working well! The first person to jump out on a branch and tell HQ that it might not be working as well as they think is crucified because, "No one else seems to be having the problem." Ignoring how delicate this situation can be will kill you. You must address this very gingerly. You need someone in the organization to tell you what he or she wants. The people in the trenches want products and services that help them get the job done. The people in the ivory tower also want products and services that help their people get the job done.

This seems pretty simple until you consider the politics in place within a large organization. The people in the trenches won't tell you that they want something if it puts them at risk. Upper management won't tell you that they want something if they're not aware of the problem. I call it collective corporate denial. Even if you've personally exhumed a problem, upper management won't recognize it, and the people in the trenches will deny it leaving you smack dab in the middle of no-man's land. That's a really dangerous place to be.

Scenario 2, The Kevorkian Factor

Dr. Jack Kevorkian is the infamous and controversial doctor who helped many terminally ill people end their lives after learning that they had a terminal illness. It's known as assisted suicide. The theory is that people would prefer to die now with dignity than to suffer a slow agonizing death. I'm not here to argue for or against it, but I'm struck by how badly it's needed in modern business. Time marches on. Programs that once worked very well no longer apply, but the people who were applauded for creating them just won't let go. In a large company, there may be dozens, even hundreds of people employed in virtually redundant positions or departments. In extreme cases, these situations are not just redundant, they're counter-productive or downright destructive. Many of those people know that the end is imminent, but they realize that the result of convincing HQ will be the demise of their career. So they keep showing up every day until the company can no longer deny what has become painfully obvious. Resources are no longer committed to the program or department, as it dies a slow and agonizing death. People in this position want a solution. They need a solution. But searching for a solution requires acknowledging a problem that will cost them their jobs!

Scenario 3, If It Were That Great an Idea, I Would Have Thought of It!

You will occasionally meet aggressive individuals within organizations who are recognized as change agents. It's exciting when you make a sales call on an aggressive, forward thinking, and dynamic buyer. Sometimes these people are open minded because they genuinely want to know what's out there so that they can continue to find ways to be better. Unfortunately this is not always the case. Everyone wants to be in a position to control his or her own destiny. Some of the buyers you'll meet will consider you to be a threat if you are able to expose a problem that they overlooked. You will really be a threat to these persons if you find a simple answer to a problem that they have been unable to fix. Once you're viewed as a threat, you're done. Everything you propose will be shot down. Go over this person's head, and he or she will become a sniper in the weeds waiting for an opportunity to assassinate you. You may be successful in convincing his or her boss to give you a try against this buyer's recommendation. Once you do, this buyer will find ways to prove that you can't do what you said you could do and that choosing you was a mistake. No matter how effective your solution might be, if a key person in the organization is determined to make it fail, it will. Decidedly few things in sales are as frustrating as knowing that you can help someone who refuses to let you.

Dealing with It—

In each of these cases, you are considered a threat. Going over the sniper's head is the worst thing you can do! It will work if and only if the higher-ranking person you go to is already aware of this individual's shortcomings. It's elementary corporate politics. What this person really wants is to be in control. You need to build trust with this person even though you genuinely don't want to. If he or she drives the decision, they're not going to jump in the back and let you drive unless they really like where you want to take them and they trust that you have the skill to take them there. If the place you want to take them involves surrendering control of their destiny, they simply will not want to go.

13. The Adoption Curve.

There are people who strive to have the newest, latest, most advanced product available. Initial bugs don't bother them, it's part of the deal. These people expect to pay a premium to be the first on the block. They typically won't tell us that, but it's easy enough to figure out by looking around. Notice what kind of computer, watch, tie, car, they own. Engage in some strategic small talk about hobbies and interests. If they have photos on the wall or on the desk, take a look at them. If you get the sense that your prospect appreciates the latest and greatest, be aware of the impact that it will have on his or her buying habits. Companies invest large sums of money developing new technologies and new products. The earliest buyers pay for most of this R&D in the high initial cost of the product. Once the R&D is paid, the price comes down, and the masses jump on board. There are a select few buyers who will not purchase until the product has been out long enough to work out the bugs. By then, the price is very low. These late adopters may not come out and tell you that they're still waiting because there is increasing pressure on the few remaining people who don't have the item. Pocket calculators are a great example of this.

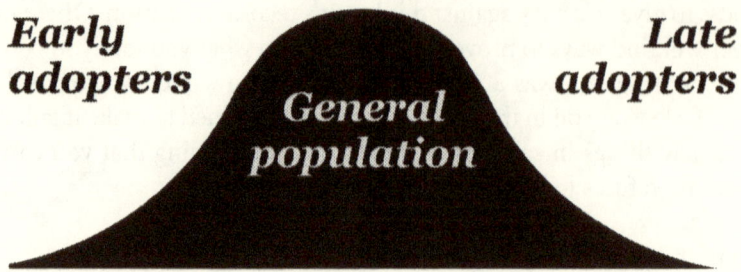

Early adopters

General population

Late adopters

Since price has factored into most of the above scenarios, let's talk a little bit about price. If you're thinking that price means strictly currency, dollars, and cents, then you've missed the point. Money was created for the sole purpose of simplifying and standardizing the barter process. When you spend money, you are deciding to forego anything else that you could have purchased with the money that you no longer have. Money represents the freedom to choose. The monetary price, therefore, is not just the paper and metal that we call money; it's the freedom to choose. I've always found perplexing that we all want the freedom of choice in spite of the pain associated with having to choose.

Determining what your prospects really want can be tough. Unfortunately, success in sales depends upon your ability to do it. When you say you tried to find out what they want, you're saying you failed. Saying that you gave it an honest effort is simply not good enough. In the words of Yoda, the sage from the Star Wars saga, "Do or do not, there is no try." So many salespeople try it briefly, then get frustrated and go straight to price. For a career in sales, that move signals the beginning of the end.

Dealing with it—

You must get to know your prospect well enough to know where he or she falls on the adoption curve. If you're trying to generate interest in new and improved products, be sure it's to an early adopter. If you're selling to a late adopter, stick with the tried and true.

3

Selling Is More than Dollars and Cents.

"What we obtain too cheap, we esteem too lightly."
—Thomas Paine

What Is the purpose of Your Job?

If you answered, "The purpose of my job is to make sales," you will not succeed. Making sales is the *goal* of your job. The *purpose* of your job is to solve customer problems. Many salespeople get this wrong, and they pay a very dear price. If you believe the purpose of your job is to make sales, you'll focus on what *you* want. That's a funny thing about focus. If you focus on what you want, you'll be blind to what *your prospect* wants. This section addresses the single most important component in the selling process. I can't tell you how many times I've seen a salesperson so focused on his or her own wants that they didn't even hear their prospect when he or she told them what they wanted.

How Low Can You Go?

Price inevitably plays a role in every sale. So what is your product or service worth? Simply put, *free* really isn't cheap enough! When you ask your prospect to give you something like money, you must give them something back such as your company's products or services. If they don't perceive what they're getting to be of greater value than what they have to give up, they'll say no every time. It's not good enough to be of equal value either. If I walk into your home and ask you to give me a five-dollar bill in exchange for me giving you a five-dollar bill, what's the point of that? Who has time for that? On the other hand, if I ask for a five-dollar bill in exchange for something that you feel is worth six-dollars, now we're talking.

This sounds so basic and elementary, yet I am dumbfounded at how many salespeople seem to do this wrong. Here's what they typically miss. Your product or service has no intrinsic value. It does not matter how much it cost for you to produce or provide it. It matters not that someone else was willing to buy it or how much that other person was willing to pay for it. The key to pricing is this: Your product or service is worth whatever that specific customer is willing to pay for it. If you are asking your prospect to change suppliers, ideally you will have created enough value in their mind to justify why your product or service is worth more. Barring that, you must convince your prospect that they will be happier with it at the same price as their current supplier. If your product or service needs to be cheaper in order to earn the business, you probably haven't done your job.

Infomercial Selling

It slices, it dices, it's guaranteed not to rust, bust, or gather dust, and it makes mounds of julienne fries! *Now how much would you pay? Wait, don't answer yet, there's more!* And if you call in the next 20 minutes, you'll receive this bonus! The next time you see a commercial on television, notice the order in which the process takes place.

1. They demonstrate what it can do.
2. They do everything they can think of to get you to want it.
3. They list several reasons why it is, logically, a smart decision (They help you to rationalize the decision).
4. They compare it to similar products both in terms of performance and cost.
5. They illustrate the capabilities so that you become concerned that you might not be able to afford it since, with all that's going for it, it's likely to be very expensive. You start to envision a number in your mind that you anticipate the price is likely to be.
6. Finally, after you've decided that you want it *and* need it, but fear that with all those extras it has to be a lot more than you're willing to spend, they give the price. If the price is lower than you expected it to be, you decide to buy because it is a good value. You have determined that the benefits of what you're getting outweigh what you have to give up in order to get it.

Price must always be the last piece of the puzzle. It must only be presented after you've convinced your prospect that it's worth more than the price you're about to share with them.

If you are successful in creating strong desire in the buyer's heart, he or she will embrace the logic used to support the decision and downplay logical arguments against it. If you try to address the needs logically prior to capturing the buyer's heart, the buyer will begin to spar with you. In sales, we call these objections or obstacles. And price is the ultimate obstacle. Take a critical look at the TV commercials. Without fail, the best commercials will always capture your heart first. You will see images of people living the life you want to live. If the cost is even mentioned, it is always *after* they've done everything they can think of to get you to want the product.

You must present your case in precisely this sequence and here's why. Every buyer will go through three distinct phases when considering a purchase. The first phase involves curiosity and desire. Cost, a rational and logical argument is not yet a concern in this early phase, so why make it one. As salespeople, we need to stoke the embers of desire as we go after the heart. It does not matter how much it costs if the buyer has no desire. Once desire is established, the buyer will move into phase two, evaluating alternatives. Whatever you're selling will be gauged against any other product or service that might fit the bill. Cost is still not a primary concern. The buyer in this phase is trying to determine what else may be available to address this desire. The third and last phase of the buying process is cost. In these final moments the buyer is deciding whether your product or service is worth the sacrifice. If you have not sufficiently piqued the interest by this point, it's probably too late.

The Price Is Too High!

Even if you've done everything right, you're still going to hear it. That's why so many salespeople stop going through the effort. Mediocre salespeople will say, "If it always comes down to price, why bother with the rest of the nonsense?" In order to overcome the dreaded price obstacle, you must look past "The price is too high!" Before you give up and drop your price, don't automatically assume that they have a lower price from somewhere else and that the price is all that matters. Determine what your prospect is really saying. Here are a few thoughts.

The smokescreen

It's possible that they just don't have the money. "Your price is too high" is not as embarrassing as saying "I just can't afford it." Your customers and prospects may be forced to make drastic budget cuts, particularly when economic times are tight. Where they used to look for a total package of value, they may now be looking for anyone who can give them a low no-frills price that they can take to their boss and say, "Look what I did!" In tough times, your customer or prospect's primary motivation may be to survive the next round of lay-offs.

If you suspect this to be the case, examine your complete offering and ask your customer if there is anything they can live without to help you cut costs in order to justify a lower price. Doing this accomplishes four important things.

➢ It gives you an opportunity to remind your customer about everything you do that your low-priced competitor may not do.
➢ It serves as a reality check. You may think you're worth more only to find that your package of value contains benefits that your customers enjoy but aren't willing to pay for.

> ➤ It preserves your integrity. Anytime you reduce the price without some compromise by the customer, you're planting seeds of doubt that you might previously have been ripping them off.
> ➤ A "lite" program may cost you substantially less to provide than the complete package. This allows you to meet a lower-price offering and still maintain profitability. In some cases you may actually improve the bottom line.

Beware! If your prospect's financial solvency is the real issue at hand, you might get burned.

"I know you believe you understand what you think I said. But I'm not sure that you realize that what you heard is not what I meant!"

Your prospect may be convinced that he or she can get the exact same quality product or service at a lower price. You must demonstrate to your customer the features and benefits of your complete package that make this a superior value specific to their needs. A word of caution: Be careful not to list features or benefits that don't apply directly to your customer. Doing so will have several profound negative consequences.

> ➤ You risk overselling. Customers tell themselves "No wonder you're more expensive; I'm paying for all these features I don't need."
> ➤ By listing features that don't apply, you risk having the prospect feel as if you don't really know him or her as well as they thought you did. Any major sale requires a connection between the buyer and the seller. Your prospect must believe that you understand his or her situation, care enough to help, and can provide solutions to their challenges.
> ➤ What you're selling as a benefit may actually raise concerns as a negative. If you were selling homes and started talking about quiet peaceful surroundings due to the distance from the city, you might be raising concerns about the length of the commute. If the buyer did not have children, and you went into great detail about the great school system, they might become concerned about property taxes.

To demonstrate your strengths, avoid vague lip service. Casual comments like "We're the best..." or "Our service is superior..." are worthless! Just for fun, ask your customer or prospect how many salespeople stop in to call on them each week. Then ask how many claim to be the best!

When describing your strengths, do not blast the competitor. Doing so just reveals insecurity, and it insults your prospect. After all, the person you're working with may be the one who chose them, and your competitor must do a pretty good job or your prospect would have been sharp enough to switch before now. Instead, compliment your competitor. Your approach should sound something like, "They're a fine outfit; we compete against them pretty regularly. Here's what they do well, and here's how we do it even better!" Testimonials or referrals from a few of their customers who now buy from you are worth their weight in gold!

You need to know what you're up against. Don't be afraid to tell your prospect that you'd like to review your offer and talk to others in your organization to see what might be possible. So that you can be fully prepared when discussing the opportunity, there are a few questions that need to be answered.

> What, precisely, has your competitor proposed?
> Has your competitor guaranteed to outperform, or was it lip service?
> What does your prospect like or dislike about your competitor's offering other than the price?
> What does your prospect like or dislike about your offering?
> What has he or she heard about your product, your company, or you personally?
> Does your prospect think your competitor's offering and your offering are essentially identical?
> Are they identical?

Until your make absolutely certain that your customer is comparing apples to apples, you'll never stand a chance!

"Go away kid, you bother me"—W.C. Fields

Picture yourself in your prospect's shoes. If he or she has been doing this for any length of time, he or she is likely to have see dozens, maybe even hundreds of salespeople. Each salesperson vows to lead them to the Promised Land. "What's your price?" is the quickest way to weed out the amateurs without being rude. They ask your price, you tell them, they say you're too high. You say let me see what I can do and you go away! It works! Furthermore, if the buyer is sophisticated, you're likely to hear during subsequent visits, "Your price is getting close." The prospect gives you a glimmer of hope while beating you down as far as you're willing to go. He or she will take that price to their current supplier and threaten to take away their business. Your prospect uses you to beat up their current supplier, and your competitor is the one forced to defend his or her price, which can take place through any of these strategies.

Standard Operating Procedure

Most prospects will try to beat you down at first even if your price is the lowest. Sophisticated buyers have figured out that your first price is rarely your bottom price, so they beat you down as a matter of course. If your first price was your bottom price, what were you thinking? While I'm not inclined to distill an entire course on negotiating down to a paragraph or two, it's critically important that you start high. Each time that you move from the price, the margin should get smaller. You might start with a 5 percent discount, than 2 percent, then a fraction of a percent. When you approach the figure where you hope to stop, work the price in terms of uneven pennies (i.e. $1600.00, $1520.00, $1490.00, then finally $1,484.27). It gives the impression that you must be getting close or you would round off. Don't assume that you'll automatically get the business when your price finally inches below the competition. If you've been moving down with each pass, a savvy prospect will keep pushing until you stop moving even if your first price was good enough. And don't automatically assume that you'll get the business with a super low price. Your prospect might show your quote to your competitor before changing suppliers, just to see how badly they want to hang on to the business. That's why you never, ever go to the bottom. If your competitor drops his or her price trying to keep the business, you'll need to have some room to move. Once your prospect gets their price lowered by your competitor, he or she can't help but feel a little bit ripped off. They'll wonder "I've been loyal to them for a long time. Why did I have to threaten to leave in order to get their best deal?"

Don't Sweat the Small Stuff

If you're selling an array of products or services to a prospect, never quote them all at once. Your greatest profit opportunity lies in the ancillary products, not in the core products. If you've ever purchased a computer printer, you've been exposed to this principle. Buyers head to the computer store with a price range in mind. Once they narrow the field down to products within this range, they compare features such as speed, resolution, size, and paper capacity. You will not see the price of the replacement ink or toner cartridge near the printer display. Printer manufacturers have figured out that they can lose money on the sale of the printer because they'll make it back ten-fold on the sale of cartridges. Yet, when making the purchase, surprisingly few buyers are sensitive to the cost of replacement cartridges.

Early in the negotiation, your prospect will be sensitive to pricing on a few key items just to see if you're worth talking to. This is important. Your goal is to present as few items as possible, start high, and let them beat you up just enough to get you close, but not far enough to be below your competitor. You need them to say that you're still a bit high so that you have an opportunity to explain why you are worth more. Once those prices are in the ballpark, you'll get past the price obstacle and be given the opportunity to present your complete package of value. They may beat you up from there, but you won't have to drop as low. In addition, you can make up some of the lost profit with those ancillary items that were not part of this negotiation. Depending on your industry, you may want to save some of those smaller items to throw in as a bonus, pushing the major items over the top when negotiations reach an impasse.

Ideally, you will present a price on one or two pieces of the business and let them get their need for hard negotiating out of their system. Make sure you started high enough and made the negotiation rigorous enough so that your prospect, the buyer, feels like they gave their employer due diligence. When you discuss the little stuff later, you can ask, with chagrin, "Man, you wore me out on the last round. You're going to beat me up on this little stuff too?" While you may eventually be asked to fill in the blanks with quotes on additional items, I have never, and I mean NEVER had a prospect require pricing on every single product or service prior to making the decision to use me as a supplier.

It's a specific sequence of events. First, the buyer requests a price quote either to blow you off or to see if you're worth talking to. Then you come back with high prices on a piece of the business and allow them beat you down to where you're a smidgeon higher. Next you justify why you're worth at least that much more. If you reach an impasse and you have some small bonus you can throw in that's worth more to your prospect than it costs you to provide, now is the time to offer it.

Some buyers will make it a point to beat their suppliers up on an annual basis just to be sure that they aren't leaving money on the table. This is another good reason for keeping a few insignificant prices high so that you have some room to negotiate down the road.

We Have Top Quality and Low Prices, Which One Did You Want?

If you started high, your prospect will inevitably want to know why you're more expensive. This is an engraved invitation to describe all of the advantages your company has to offer. When told, "Your price is too high…" don't be afraid to say, "Yes! We are typically more expensive, and here's why…" Doing this will position your company as the premium supplier. If you later have to reduce the price, you may only need to move a little bit closer to matching the competitor's price. You may not have to beat it. You want your customer to think, "If I can get all that for about the same money, I'm interested."

The Price, in and of Itself, Means Very Little

Suppose you were shopping for a home and you wanted a good deal. In your search, you talked to one person who was selling a 3-bedroom home for $100,000 and another person who was selling a 3-bedroom home for

$120,000. Let's further assume that they were similar in terms of size and age. If you were focused on price and price alone, you might be leaning toward the $100,000 home. Now suppose the $120,000 home overlooked a private lake, had all new premium appliances and was in the best school district. The $100,000 home was really beat up, was in a bad neighborhood and did not come with appliances. Furthermore, it overlooked the county landfill and backed up to railroad tracks. This example is painfully obvious. How does it compare to what you sell? Do you fully illustrate all of the features other than price that will influence the decision? With any proposal, there is always more than price. Remember that there are four basic elements to any proposal.

> ➤ What will your prospect get that they want?
> ➤ What will they get that they don't want?
> ➤ What will they have to give up (that they want) in order to get it?
> ➤ What will they be able to get rid of (that they don't want) if they get it?

It gets right back to the four keys to motivation mentioned earlier. If choosing to buy the second home means you will get some things that you want (new premium appliances, good school district, great view) and avoid some things you don't want (smell from the landfill, noise from the train, potential crime from the neighborhood) you may choose it even if you have to give up something that you want like the additional $20,000. Each person will weigh all of those features and reach a decision. The problem in most selling situations is that the salesperson leaves it to the prospect to vaguely compare and contrast each aspect of the decision. Decision criteria tend to get foggy when left vague. If the decision gets foggy, the risk of overlooking something important becomes paramount in the decision.

Think about it. Your prospect must feel comfortable that you've told him or her all the positive reasons for making the change. Indecision is caused by concerns or problems that they might have overlooked. That's why I call it *foggy*. When asked to move forward into the fog, your prospect will be nervous about what might be out there that he or she can't see.

Be absolutely certain you've fully illustrated each and every pertinent difference between your offering and your competition *including your competition's strengths!* Then explain why yours is a better value. Make sure that it's specific to your prospect's circumstances, then stand your ground! Your prospect may not find another supplier at a lower price that can meet all of their criteria. In order for this to work, two critical conditions must be met:

> ➤ You must really know your prospect's wants and needs.
> ➤ You must know your competitor inside out.

If these two conditions are not met, your strategy will amount to little more than rolling the dice and hoping for a seven. Even if you win the sale, you'll almost certainly leave some money on the table.

You Started It!

Sometimes, your customer is telling you that your price is too high because you unwittingly invited him to. Here's how it happens. Picture going into a department store to buy a new outfit. When you ask how much the suit is, the salesman says, "$500, but I can sell it to you for $450." Then you ask how much the shirt costs, and he says, "Normally $75, but I can sell it to you for $50." When you ask about the tie and he says $50, you are likely to ask, "How much can you sell me that for?" as if expecting a discount. From that point forward, you have been conditioned to expect a discount on everything in the store even if the original price was competitive! Then, when you don't get something taken off the price, you feel sore! Here's the right way. When asked, "How much is the suit?" the salesman should have responded, "$500," and shut up. If you weren't comfortable with the price, you might ask for a discount. If he were a pro, the salesman would have gone to some effort to justify the price first by describing durability, quality, style or any distinguishing features that made it worth more. Then, when he provided a discount, he might have justified the price break by saying something like, "I can offer you a discount on the suit if you buy the shirt and tie from me at the same time." In this way, the salesman is conditioning his customer to give something in return. This will shut the discount spiral down cold.

Selling a Commodity

Successfully defending a higher price is impossible when your prospect sees no difference between your offering and your competitor's offering. Most of us have been in a sales situation where the product that your prospect is currently buying is a product that you also sell. By far the worst thing you can do is to tell them you carry the exact same product and ask how much they are paying for it. Once you've done that, you've reduced the sale to price and price alone. Not only does it send a clear signal to your prospect that you have nothing else to offer, but continually battling on price alone will almost certainly initiate a price war. When you drop your price, profit margins get compressed. That will erode your company's ability to provide the service and infrastructure that differentiates you. Over time, your company's capabilities become diminished, and you'll have nothing to sell except for price. As your competitor struggles to respond, they will feel the same effects. In order to replace the revenue you cost them, they're likely to go after your accounts with a stupid price. In retaliation, you go after their best accounts with the same approach. A vicious circle ensues. In short, you lose, and your competitor loses. At the bottom, you and your competition are so focused on killing each other with price that quality and service suffer. When your customer can no longer depend on you or your competitor to provide the quality and service he or she needs, your customer loses. Unless there is a reason why your company enjoys a genuine and substantial cost advantage, a price war is a lose-lose-lose situation.

Subtract price from the equation and ask yourself how your company clearly differentiates itself from the competition? If your company's product or service does not clearly differentiate from your competition, the salesperson must determine how he or she clearly differentiates from the competitor's salesperson. In simple terms, if the product or service cannot differentiate from its competition, the salesperson must be the difference. If he or she quits and goes to the competition, the business typically follows. Companies learn that if you want that account, hire that salesperson. Because the salesperson becomes as great a threat as a value to his or her employer, they are well compensated. That's where you want to be; that's where a career in selling really gets good. Yet so many salespeople spend their lives looking for a product or service that's easier to sell. Just remember, if it were easy, anyone could do it.

Sales success rests on your ability and diligence to make a lot of calls early to identify customers that will embrace the difference you represent—weeding out and not wasting time on those that won't—and your ability to uncover, develop and sell the customer on those differences.

Your Price Might Be Too Low!

You might laugh out loud, but believe it or not, your price can be too low. While everyone wants a good value, a quality conscious buyer will be very skeptical if your price is substantially lower than your competition. You've heard the phrase, "If something sounds too good to be true, it probably is." I remember working a retail counter at a tire store many years ago. A customer came in looking for an original equipment replacement tire for his Mercedes Benz. When I quoted the low price, he looked genuinely surprised and asked if it were a blemished tire or a factory second. I explained that it was precisely the same product he would buy anywhere. He said he'd think about it and left. About an hour later, the local Mercedes Benz dealership called me to buy the same set of tires. The dealership bought it from us for the same price offered directly to the car's owner. They marked it up an additional $50 per tire and sold them to the same guy that had stopped in to see me earlier. Because they did not have the equipment to properly install the tires, they wrapped the tires in plastic bags, then placed them in the trunk and back seat. The owner of the car drove back to the tire store and paid even more to have the tires installed. The message is clear. At the higher price, the tires were more in line with what he expected to pay. He made the purchase with more confidence that it was the high quality product he was looking for. It's one more sound reason for starting high when quoting: They just might say yes. When you hear, "Your price is too high," you have an opportunity to describe the key benefits about your company that make you worth more. I'll go so far as to say that if you don't hear it, your odds of making the sale go down!

Some Final Thoughts on Price

Beyond those things that money can buy are all the things that money cannot buy. When you are considering the cost involved in a decision, you must consider peace of mind, risk, ridicule, physical pain, time, relationships, health, happiness, and so much more.

The price may be as simple as having to ask the boss for permission. Even if your prospect knows it's best, he or she may be so intimidated by their supervisor that the thought of asking for permission to switch suppliers is terrifying and is too high a price to pay. There's an added dynamic if your contact person inherited the current vendor. If the incumbent fails, your contact can blame his or her predecessor. If your contact fights to bring you in as a replacement and something goes wrong, it's his or her fault. The price may be telling their current supplier to go away. If your prospect has been buying from that supplier for some time, there's likely to be a personal connection. For some, causing hurt feelings is too high a price to pay. Consider the scale in the following illustration. When determining the price, visualize every factor that might be on either tray. If the scale leans gently toward the left, you're making progress. If it drops dramatically to the left, the sale is a slam dunk! If it gently leans to the right, there's still some work to be done. If it drops dramatically to the right, you're not even close. Think of it in these simple terms. If I give you a dollar bill and you give me back four quarters, the transaction was a wash; the quarters were essentially free. If I give you a dollar bill and you give me back five quarters, I'm better off than when I started. Every sales transaction involves your customer giving you something in exchange for your giving them something. If what they get is worth as much TO THEM as what they give you, the transaction was free. If what they get is worth more TO THEM, they're ahead of the game.

Remember that there are four ways to tip the scales.

Whether you're giving your prospect something that they want (such as improved features and benefits) or helping them to lose something that they don't want (like breakdowns), you're tipping the scale toward a yes. Conversely, when you give them something that they don't want (like a confrontation with the boss) or causing them to lose something that they want (money in the bank or a long-term relationship with their current supplier), you're tipping toward a no.

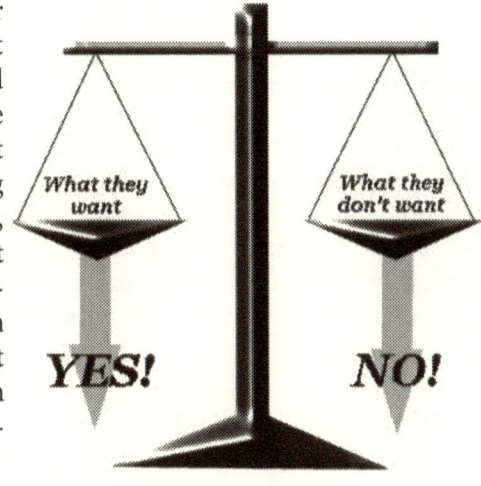

What Is Needed,  **What Is Wanted**

"Half the mistakes in life arise from feeling where we ought to think, and thinking where we ought to feel."

—*John Churton Collins*

Tremendous difficulty arises when the need and the want are conflicting. Recall that a need is a logical argument that resides in the head. A want is an emotional argument that resides in the heart. These decisions can be paralyzing, and here's why. You can logically explain all the reasons for doing something that you need to do, but don't want to do. A want is an emotional argument that does not respond to logic. This is why people procrastinate. Everyone will agree that when you have something really important that needs to get done, you should do it right away and get it over with. Yet so many people find 101 less important things to do instead. Why? Because, while they know they need to, they just don't want to do it. The need and the want are conflicting. Conversely, you may know deep down in your heart that there is something you want, and you won't be happy until you get it. But emotions can rarely be verbalized in such a way that they can be used to debate logically. You feel torn in two directions, and the result is often a stalemate also known as procrastination. That's where rationalization comes in.

Rationalization

"The moment we want to believe something, we suddenly see all the reasons for it, and become blind to the arguments against it."—George Bernard Shaw

I urge you to read this section carefully, then take some time to digest it. Whether or not you realize it, you're doing it every day. You're probably not even aware that you're doing it, and it's having a profound impact on your life! To become truly successful in sales (and generally in life), you will need to thoroughly understand rationalization. Rationalization, used positively, can assist you in reaching your goals. Used negatively it will dash any hopes of reaching them.

Is Rationalization Good or Bad?

Any decision, good or bad, can be rationalized if the desire is strong enough! Through rationalization, want will drive need. If there's a need without a corresponding want, rationalization may be used to undo it. Deciding whether or not you agree with rationalization is immaterial. Rationalization is a fact of life. It would be like deciding whether or not you agree with gravity.

Each of us needs to justify all of our behavior rationally. If we can't, we are being irrational. Irrational is really another word for insane, crazy, or just plain nuts. Isn't that what insanity really is? When a person does something and can't provide a logical, rational reason for why he or she did it, they're considered crazy.

If you ask someone why he or she is doing something, the answer will always fall into one of only two categories. It will be emotional or it will be rational. Occasionally, it will be a combination of the two. The emotional response is, "Because I wanted to," or "It felt like the right thing to do at the time." Emotional responses address instincts and feelings. The rational response will attempt to assign logical reasoning and sound something like, "It made sense for the following reasons," or "It provided the following benefits." In the business world, decidedly few people are admired for making decisions based on their feelings. The only people who are even given the luxury of acting from their instincts are owners, CEOs, or key leaders in the organization; and there's good reason for that. Large companies cannot have hundreds or thousands of employees each doing their job their own way based upon what "feels" right without having to justify their actions? It would be a disaster. Leaders must be able to depend on their staffs to implement their vision in a dependable and structured manner. As Jonathan Swift once said, "Vision is the art of seeing the invisible." Having the vision to determine strategic direction defies logic and requires intuition. Once determined, structure and discipline are required in order to implement and carry out the vision. If you want to read more on methods for solid logical implementation, I urge you to read the works of W. Edwards Deming.

Rationalization is the process of taking a want, which is emotional, and justifying it logically, or rationally turning it into a need so that you feel better about doing it. Read that last sentence again and notice how paradoxical it is.

➤ You *feel* like doing something
➤ You *justify* why it's logically a good idea so that you *feel* better about doing it.

The same process works in reverse.

➤ There's something you *don't feel* like doing.
➤ You *rationalize* why doing it is a bad idea so that you feel better about *not doing* it.

That's why you must capture the heart first. If you do, rationalization will be used to justify doing what you propose. If you don't, your prospect will use rationalization to justify not doing what you propose. According to *Webster's*, to rationalize is "to invent plausible explanations for actions that are actually based on less acceptable causes." Years of societal programming have given us a tremendous amount of guilt when we say we did something simply because we wanted to. It's much easier to justify doing something because we needed to. This may sound like a contradiction, but it's not.

Allow me to give you a real-life example. I recently went shopping with my daughter to buy a car. By the way, I was paying for the car. The salesman at the first dealership kept asking my daughter what we needed in a car. Within just a few minutes, it became clear that this salesperson was not trying to explore and understand the desires or needs of the ultimate decision maker, me! More importantly, neither of us saw any vehicle on the lot that was particularly exciting, so neither of us went into much detail about needs. The salesman made no attempt to learn what we wanted, the process hit a wall, and we left. Like the mediocre majority, this salesman knew that we would eventually need to logically rationalize the decision on a large purchase like a new car. And, like the mediocre majority, he failed to capture either of our hearts first. I wanted to buy a car that she would love, and I wanted to financially impact the rest of the family as little as possible. At the next dealership, we saw a car that she simply adored. On a lot with hundreds of cars, I knew instantly which one she would be drawn to. She went right to it as we got out of the car. Of course, my first look at the car was the right side window with the price sticker. My first desire, to get her a car that she loved, was satisfied immediately. It was love at first sight. My second desire was another matter. It was significantly more expensive than any of the cars at the first dealership. The salesman's first question got right to the point, "Who will be paying for this car?" When he learned that the answer was me, he proceeded to ask what *I* wanted to find. Figuring out that she wanted this car and that I'd love to get it for her was obvious even to the casual observer. All that remained was to provide me with the rationalization I needed to justify the decision. The previous sentence bears repeating, since it is at the core of the selling process: *"All that remained was to provide me with the rationalization I needed to justify the decision."* The salesman knew this, and I helped him do it. We talked about warranties, dealership service capabilities, incentives and safety features. These are the things I "needed." First we wanted it, then the salesman helped convince me that, not only did we want it, but we all needed it. Justifying it to my daughter was irrelevant. She loved the car and didn't have to pay for it. Justifying it to my wife or myself was going to be a little tougher since we were not likely to share my daughter's enthusiasm toward the vehicle. Rationalizing the decision meant we had to come up with more acceptable reasons such as the tremendous deal, the special finance offer, the safety and dependability, the comfortable seats, dual air bags, front wheel drive and traction control and rebates. These were all good logical, rational reasons for this being a smart purchase. The fact that the car was cool was secondary and was minimized in the process.

"I swear to God, it's not my fault."
—*John Belushi (The Blues Brothers)*

When you can't land that tough prospect and you tell your boss that the buyer must be accepting bribes from your competitor, you're rationalizing. It's a plausible explanation that you would rather believe than to accept that fact that you don't have the skills to beat out your competitor. When you can't grow sales because you spend a lot of time with your existing customers instead of your prospects, you're rationalizing. You start by saying that your existing customers are very demanding and ask "What's the point in signing new business if you're going to lose what you already have in order to get it?" That's rationalizing. You're inventing plausible explanations for actions that are actually based on less acceptable causes. More likely, you're much more comfortable with your current customers, and you just don't like making cold calls.

I could go on forever with examples of rationalizations. We all rationalize throughout the day, every day. Convincing someone else that your logical reasons are valid is one thing. When you start convincing yourself, it becomes dangerous. We all do it, and we've been doing it for so long that most of us aren't even aware that we're doing it. Eventually we get so good at it that it becomes natural. Over time, it becomes difficult to determine if your reasons are sound or if you're just rationalizing.

It takes a great deal of confidence and courage to stand up and say to the world, "I messed up," "I can't do it," or "I failed." But it's okay to fail as long as you learn from it. Henry Ford once said, "Failure is simply the opportunity to begin again, this time more intelligently." But if something goes wrong and you can't accept the notion that it happened because you failed, you will invent a different explanation. You won't learn from it, and you won't grow.

Changing What Your Prospect Wants

"How many psychiatrists does it take to change a light bulb? Only one but it has to really want to be changed!"—Dr. Phil

If you don't have what they want, you cannot change what they want. Barring genuine interest in their product or service, salespeople often commit another fatal mistake. They try to make their prospect change what they want and it rarely works. Try as you might, if your prospect doesn't want to change, you can't make him or her do it. Trying to make your prospect want your product is an approach that far too many salespeople attempt and fail. After they fail to make their prospect want it, they try to make their prospect agree to buy it logically. They are then surprised when the prospect presents a myriad of insurmountable objections. They become so frustrated that they buy and read books on how to overcome objections. WRONG! If you're doing this, please stop! If your prospect deep down does not want what you're selling, he or she will continue to provide objections until you eventually give up and go away. If the price tag is small enough, you may wear them down until they eventually agree to buy from you just to make you go away. If this is the case, I hope you have an unlimited number of new prospects to choose from, because eventually, these people will become conspicuously tough to see. If you've made it to the point where your prospect says, "Look, I just don't want it," you've made progress. Unfortunately, by that point, your prospect is tired of dealing with you and you won't move forward.

If you've exposed desire and your prospect is voicing concerns, he or she is probably looking for you to help them rationalize the decision. This is a great place to be because you and your prospect want the same thing. You just need to work together to figure out how to make it happen. Concerns are not the same as objections. They are polar opposites. Objections are roadblocks presented by your prospect to keep you from reaching your destination (the sale).

The more force you use to blast through each roadblock, the more formidable each subsequent objection will become. Eventually, your prospect will present one that you just can't get through. Frequently but not exclusively, that final obstacle is the price. Objections point toward specifics. Concerns are very different. Concerns are like road signs indicating what you need to do to get there. Concerns are presented to help you get to your destination because your prospect wants you to. If you and your prospect want the same thing, he or she will help you.

How can you tell if you're getting objections or concerns? To the untrained ear, they sound similar, but they are very different. First, objections tend to bounce around from one very specific issue to the next. Solve one, and another will pop up. Solve the second, and a third will pop up, and so on. Each time the objection may get a little more far-fetched, and the prospect will challenge your response. If you hear your prospect say "Yeah, but,…" chances are good you're about to get another objection. If you've made it past several objections and the conversations spins back around to an earlier objection, stop. Overcoming each is of little value.

Concerns have a very different sound to them, and you must listen closely. Instead of "That won't work," you'll hear, "Tell me how that would work?" Here, it's helpful to pay close attention to non-verbal communication. If "Tell me how that would work," sounds sarcastic, they're really saying, "That won't work." Furthermore, with concerns, you'll occasionally hear the prospect brainstorming how it might work because they want it to. Concerns don't usually bounce around. They tend to stay to the point. By design, they will likely start in general terms and get more specific as they go. This is an effort to clear away any fog.

If you're getting objections, STOP. You haven't put first things first. You are attempting to help your prospect rationalize a decision that they don't want to make. You're out of order. Find a way to quickly and comfortably end the meeting, then schedule a follow up. You need to jump out before you do any permanent damage. Review what you've learned, then come back with a fresh approach. Each time, you're really going back to the beginning to uncover desire. Until you have, don't even try to make the sale.

If you're having difficulty determining whether you just heard an objection or a concern, try exposing it with a "What if." For example, "What if I could show you how to lose weight, would you be interested?" Or, "If I could prove beyond any shadow of doubt that my selling system is superior, would you use it?" If the answer is a resounding "Yes" you are dealing with a concern. If you get, "I don't know," "Maybe," "I suppose," or anything less than a solid "Yes," you're probably dealing with an objection. For example, you ask, "If I could prove that we'll save you at least 10 percent, would you try a few as a test?" If the answer is something like, "That depends, tell me about your testing methods," then you're clearly dealing with a concern. If the response is defensive such as, "I've tried those tests before and they sound great at first, but I've never been able to collect on the guarantee," you're obviously hearing an objection. A sure sign that it is an objection is the word, *but*. "I'm overweight, BUT I feel great." "My car gets poor fuel economy, BUT I only drive it to the train station and back." "My current supplier has quality problems, BUT he's my boss's brother."

I'll say it again because it's important. Regardless of concern or objection, never blast your competitor. Your prospect may have been involved in choosing them as a supplier. When you blast your competitor, you're actually insulting your prospect by saying that he or she made a mistake! If your prospect just told you that they like the competitor, insulting them will be viewed as nothing less than a direct frontal assault on your prospect's intelligence. It's like asking "Who would be stupid enough to choose ABC Company and, worse yet, who would be stupid enough to stay with them after they learned what it's really like to buy from them?" Exposing a mistake that your prospect made is not going to help him or her want to do business with you. Furthermore, if you convince them that they made a mistake choosing that supplier, you may cause them to question their ability to choose a supplier. This might make them reluctant to choose you! When your prospect admits that he or she goofed when they chose the current supplier, he or she needs to save face. You need to help them do it. When you tell them that choosing your competitor was a logical decision based upon information available at the time, you earn trust. More importantly, you begin the process of getting your prospect to want to buy from you, and you reinforce their ability to make sound decisions. Your prospect will feel that you understand and appreciate them. You're always better off saying something along the lines of "We know they do this well; we watch them very carefully. We've learned that we can supply our customers with an even better solution to these challenges by taking it a step further and doing this...." Of course, you must really know your competition inside out and be able to compare and contrast your capabilities specific to the needs of the person with whom you are speaking. Blasting a competitor is easy and weak. When a sophisticated prospect hears you do it, he or she often reduces you to amateur status, particularly if your competitor is large and well heeled. The prospect will assume you do not know them very well or that they must be getting to you. Instead, highlight changes in the marketplace, change in the competitor, or changes in your prospect's business. You will begin to illustrate why the decision may have been sound at the time, but may be due for review.

4

Mapping Out the Journey

*When you don't plan for greatness,
you plan for mediocrity.*

Why Are You Going?

When you choose a career in commission sales, there will be triumph and disappointment. There will be elation and frustration. In order to stay the course, you will need to address your own motivational needs. If you don't get what you want out of the process, you won't have the energy to persist in helping your prospects get what they want. In the chapters that follow, there will be math, lots of math. The purpose of these calculations is to very specifically define the course you will be taking from where you are now to where you want to be. Only after you have specifically defined your journey will you be able to determine whether or not you are on track. On the next page is a chart entitled "What I Want Out Of Life." Use the chart to list everything you want. A blank worksheet is provided in the back of this book. Don't worry about the first column, it will be explained later. The purpose of this exercise is to define where you are going and what exactly you're working for. This list must include all the reasons for you to jump out of bed each morning and make good things happen. The list can and should include material possessions, relationships, career hopes and dreams, fitness goals, education goals, closer relationships, whatever. Anything that is important to you. Keep the list handy and throughout each day when you think of something else, write it down. Don't overthink it, now is not the time to decide if you should or should not want it. Don't put too much thought into how grand or trivial these items should be. At this juncture, no item is too grand or too trivial. Nor is now the time to figure out what it's going to take to get it. Most importantly, now is not the time to ask yourself why you want it, just write it down. Don't hold back! This list can and should be irrational. It can be a wish list or even a dream list. Looking over the list should send you daydreaming. Someone somewhere is currently enjoying anything you can possibly think of to put on the list. Why not you? One word of guidance: Try to focus on quality of life not just standard of living.

Once you start with the list, you will already be light years ahead of the mediocre performers. Geoffry Abert is quoted as saying, "The most important thing about goals is having one." Every superstar I've met is intensely goal oriented. To a champion, "good enough" rarely is. Don't be concerned whether or not the list is complete, it never will be. Life is fluid and ever changing. Your list will be a continual work in progress. You'll start to see items that you put down on a whim never expecting to achieve, yet somehow they were accomplished years earlier. You'll see items that no longer hold interest for you because you unknowingly have achieved something even greater. Over time, this list will become a tremendous source of inspiration. Astonishingly, only a small minority of people ever write down what they want out of life for several reasons.

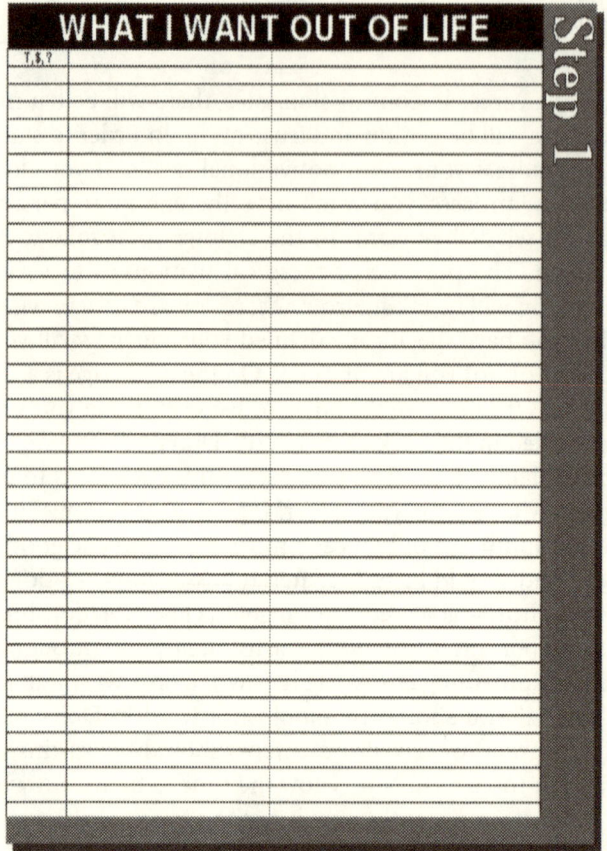

> ➤ They may have reached the comfort zone believing that they already have everything they want. How a person is raised has a tremendous impact. For someone who was raised in poverty or oppression, having a stable job, regular meals, and shelter may be their childhood definition of the good life. Funny how the terms want and need get used and abused by people who have reached their comfort zones. When you ask, "Isn't there anything you *want*?" They answer with something like "How much more do I *need*?" That's rationalization in action!

> ➤ They are too embarrassed to write it down for fear that someone might find it and laugh at the silliness. Don't ever underestimate the destructive powers of ridicule and embarrassment. Each of us can remember something embarrassing that took place many years ago. It may have taken place all the way back in childhood. Often the memory

is so clear that we become embarrassed all over again just thinking about it.

➢ Some people don't write down their desires because they're just plain lazy. I'm not talking about being too lazy to write it down—if you're too lazy too write down your goals, you're probably not going to take the time to read this book. Under-performers still spend time thinking about what they want. Just before they commit it to writing they start thinking about what it *might* require in order to achieve. Lazy people tend to understate how badly they want it while they overstate the sacrifices they'll have to make (more rationalization). The underachiever convinces himself or herself that, in the final tally, the potential costs will *probably* outweigh the potential benefits so it never makes the list. Unfortunately, if you think your head can make your heart stop wanting something, think again.

➢ This last reason is the most common and the most destructive. There's pain associated with admitting that you want something, then acknowledging that you're not going to get it. Unsuccessful people go through a great deal of effort to avoid that pain. The problem is, when these people believe that there is no way they can get it, they convince themselves that they didn't really need it (the destructive side of rationalization), so they stop trying to get it. When they stopped trying, they eliminated any chance for failure and any of the pain associated with the failure. Unfortunately, at the same time, they are erasing any opportunity for success. Picture hiking the Grand Canyon. You begin early with lots of hope and enthusiasm. You're not a sissy, so you choose a fairly challenging trail. A few hours into the journey, your leg muscles start to feel tight, but you're still feeling strong. About halfway down, you're starting to feel sore, and you stop for a little water. As you look ahead, you realize that there's still a long way to go and your muscles are even more sore than you thought they would be by this point. Then you turn to look back at what you have accomplished so far. While the awesome beauty overwhelms you, the moment of truth is fast approaching. What you start feeling deep down is, "Oh man, I still have to climb back out and every additional step I take on the way down is one more that I'll have to take on the way up! Average performers will start throwing out preliminary rationalizations. You'll hear things like "How many people on earth can even say that they've been this far?" or "Gosh, it's taken longer than anticipated to reach this point. Will we still have enough daylight to make it back up if we go all the way down? It's a great experience, but we do want to live to tell about it don't we?" Often, these types of speakers start out with a jovial tone as if they're just kidding. But they're not kidding. The seeds of rationalization are germinating, and the difference between the champions and the sea of mediocrity is at hand. Remember, to rationalize is "to invent plausible explanations for actions that are actually based on less acceptable causes." The real but less acceptable reason for turning back is either fear or laziness. But who is going to travel to Arizona, hike half way down the Grand Canyon, turn back and tell their friends that they didn't make it all the way down because they were scared or lazy? So they invent an explanation that is more acceptable to them and to whomever they hope to tell. However, the explanation must be plausible, believable. So if they can convince others, they will believe it themselves and they have a good solid excuse for turning back.

A champion eliminates excuses through commitment and courage. All the concerns voiced by the mediocre may be real, but the champion doesn't wait until he or she is half way down the canyon to think of them because, by then, it's too late. Champions have a much simpler point of view. To the champion, "I came to hike the canyon, now let's all stay focused and hike the canyon!" Champions tend to focus on the joy they will feel when they accomplish it while they tend to downplay the pain and risk. In their minds, the value exceeds the cost, and they proceed. To increase the chances of success and minimize opportunity for failure, champions are better prepared. Weeks before the hike, a champion will research the distance, time required, and supplies needed. A champion will start training weeks or even months prior to the hike. A champion will take the time to anticipate unexpected events that might occur and be prepared for them. Whether in sports, in business, or life in general, a high performance existence depends upon commitment. If you go into each day feeling like you'll give it your best shot or you'll try you are predetermining failure and you will surely fail. To a champion, failure is not an option.

Whether a champion or part of the mediocre majority, each of our hearts may get a little scared. Our nervous heart calls upon our brain for help. Our brain is more than willing to lend assistance by offering all the logical reasons why continuing is just not a smart thing to do. The mediocre rationalize and give up. Unfortunately, convincing ourselves that we are better off without something doesn't make us stop wanting it. Remember, wants come from the heart, needs from the head, and they speak different languages. Your overall quality of life will gradually diminish if you continue to suppress your desires. Why do you think so many people experience mid-life crisis? We spend years suppressing our desires convincing ourselves that we can enjoy them someday in the future. Then, somewhere between our mid-40s and 50s, we recognize our mortality, and it suddenly occurs to us that we're running out of somedays. While suppressing our desires is applauded by society as being prudent and responsible, it doesn't fill the void. The difference between a truly high-performing lifestyle and mediocrity is *not* the difference between night and day; it's usually just a matter of those toughest final minutes of darkness right before the first ray of light. Once you see the first ray, you get a burst of energy because you know that you can make it. The sense of accomplishment you get from pushing past those last few minutes tired, sore, and afraid define your character! It sounds trite, but the age-old expression, "Its always darkest right before the dawn" says it all. If you want something, go ahead and want it! Figure out what it will take to achieve, and if it's worth the price, resolve to pay the price to get it. If you honestly determine, without rationalization that what you'll have to give up is more important that what you will get, you still might want it, but you will feel better about not having it. Notice I did not say you would think it's better. I said you would feel better. Wants are about emotions, not logic.

Once you've listed everything you want out of life, you're ready for the next step. Take a close look at the list and, in general terms, think about what achieving each item will require. If there's anything on the list that you can achieve quickly and painlessly, put down the book, go out and get it right now and check it off your list. You will have accomplished your first goal. However trivial it may be, achieving a goal will give you a boost of energy. With each subsequent goal achieved, you will gain additional confidence in your ability to achieve whatever you want out of life. For the remaining items, mark which ones require money in order to be achieved by writing a $ symbol next to it. Then mark which items require time by writing a T next to it. Finally, determine which ones you don't know how to get by placing a question mark? next to it.

What you'll find is that the two greatest obstacles to achieving your goals are time and money. For many of us, that's an either/or proposition that can be maddening! Spend more time working to achieve one goal, and that's time taken away from another goal. This book is about remedying that conflict. You've heard the expression "Time is money." That's not entirely true, but it's close. It's the real conflict that we face. You spend time making money. If you had more money, you might not need to work as many hours as you do. Instead of "Time is money," I prefer thinking in terms of "Time for money," the concept of hourly wage. Hourly wage is at the core of the selling by the numbers system.

Look at your $ goals and get a general concept of how much money you'll need to earn per week to achieve them. Look again at the list and estimate how many hours you can work and still find time for your T goals. Divide the weekly earnings by the hours you plan to work. That's your hourly wage goal. Compare this to where you are right now. How much do you currently earn per week? How many hours are you currently working per week in order to earn that amount? Divide your weekly earnings by your weekly hours worked to see your current hourly wage. This does not need to be precise; we'll dive into it in great detail.

Then there are those items that simply cannot be categorized with a $ or T. Finding time to do the research may not bear fruit. Inspect them closely. These goals usually originate in the heart, not in the head. They may include finding your soul mate, raising a great kid, achieving inner peace. These are not items to be readily dismissed. Rather, they may be the most important items on your list.

When reflecting back on life, few people wish they had worked more hours, owned bigger homes, or driven more luxurious cars. What people are most likely to regret typically fall into that open category, without the $ or the T. They are often difficult to describe logically. They include things like leaving a mark on society, making the world a better place in some small way, or stopping to smell the roses. What's needed for achieving most of them is beyond the scope of this book. Most of us will still have to work. The driving force of this book is an excitement that comes from knowing that a career in sales, done properly, offers the greatest opportunity to achieve most of what you want from your life and more.

Where Will You Go?

"You got to be careful if you don't know where you're going, because you might not get there."—Yogi Berra

Using the chart in step 1, you listed what you want out of life. Then you indicated which ones require time and which require money. You reviewed the chart and approximated the annual income you will need to achieve the goals on the list. That's your personal income goal, it's "where you're going". There are 14 steps remaining, each designed to define and map out your journey. Examples are provided in the pages that follow; blank worksheets are included in the back of this book.

Your next step is to consider how long it will take to get there and how that dollar figure will be impacted by inflation. Starting with your personal income goal, add the projected increase in the cost of living over each year. The following chart is an example. This process will be more meaningful if you research what rate of inflation you can expect over the next several years in your area. Start in column A in the first row labeled "Yr 1" and write down your income goal. In column B, write the cost of living adjustment or rate of inflation you expect for the year. Multiply column A by column B to determine how much additional income you'll need to enjoy the same standard of living in year 2. Write that number in column C. In column D, add your income goal from A to the additional income needed from C to determine the total income you'll need a year from now to enjoy the same standard of living that your original income goal would buy today. We call this your adjusted income goal. Bring that number down to the next row and repeat the process. When you reach the last row, you will have calculated the total amount of income you will need in five years to enjoy the lifestyle you pictured when you determined your income goal in step 1.

Yr	A: Annual Income Goal		B: Cost of Living Adjustment		C: Additional Income Needed		D: Adjusted Income Goal
1	$100,000	X	4%	=	$4,000	A+C=	$104,000
2	$104,000	X	4%	=	$4,160	A+C=	$108,160
3	$108,160	X	4%	=	$4,326	A+C=	$112,486
4	$112,486	X	4%	=	$4,499	A+C=	$116,985
5	$116,985	X	4%	=	$4,679	A+C=	$121,664

Step 2

When you came up with your income goal, you were picturing what your life would be like when you reached that income level. Since everything you envisioned is likely to cost more each year, the lifestyle you seek will become more expensive. If inflation averages 4 percent per year as in the above example, a lifestyle that today requires a $100,000 income will require an income of over $121,000 five years from now.

Where Are You Starting From?

In these turbulent times, you just can't feel complacent. If you've been in your industry for a year or more, you are likely to have faced losing at least one customer due to circumstances that were well beyond your control. Corporate mergers, acquisitions, bankruptcies, downsizing/rightsizing, and reorganizations are rampant. Furthermore, an unprecedented number of buyers are losing their jobs, and people with loyalties to other suppliers are replacing them. Bottom line: There is business contributing to your income today that you will have to replace, and there is nothing you can do about it. In the next calculation, you'll estimate what that attrition may be.

Starting in column A of the first row, write down your current annual income. In column B, write down what percentage of your business you're likely to lose each year due to circumstances beyond your control. We call this attrition. In column C, multiply column A times column B to see how much real income dollars you are likely to lose to attrition. In column D, subtract column C from column A to see what your income is likely to be a year from now if you lose the amount of business you anticipated. Bring this number down to the first column in the next row and repeat the process. When you reach the last row, you will have calculated what your income is likely to be due to circumstances beyond your control.

It's been said that if you're standing still in a world that's moving forward, you're actually going backward. As the above example illustrates, if you currently earn $60,000 in commissions and you lose 5 percent of your business each year due to factors beyond your control, your commission income in 5 years will drop below $47,000! Every salesman who has completed this exercise with me has initially underestimated the impact.

Yr	A: Annual Income		B: Rate of attrition		C: Income Lost		D: Adjusted Income
1	$60,000	X	5%	=	$3,000	A-C=	$57,000
2	$57,000	X	5%	=	$2,850	A-C=	$54,150
3	$54,150	X	5%	=	$2,708	A-C=	$51,442
4	$51,442	X	5%	=	$2,572	A-C=	$48,870
5	$48,870	X	5%	=	$2,443	A-C=	**$46,427**

Step 3

How Far Will You Have to Go?

First you calculated where you're headed. Then you calculated your starting point. Now you can determine how far you have to go. Subtract your adjusted income calculated in step 2 from your personal income goal in step 1 to find how much additional income you will need.

In the above example, you will need to more than double your current rate of success if you want to achieve your goals. Are you depressed yet? It gets worse. But remember that knowledge is power, and you can't fix what you don't know. As painful as it may be, you must complete this exercise so that you are keenly aware of each piece of the puzzle. This "additional income needed" is a key component in the process.

Adjusted income goal from step 2		Adjusted income from step 3		Additional Income Needed	
$121,664	Subtract	**$46,427**	=	**$75,237**	Step 4

Managing "Waypoints"

Any ambitious journey will have a starting point, a destination and a collection of "waypoints." Waypoints are points along the way used to gauge your progress and keep you on schedule. It's a way of breaking a long journey into smaller, more manageable segments. If you complete each segment on schedule, you are sure to reach your destination on time. The same principle applies to any goal, especially selling. You now know where you're starting from, and you decided where you plan to go. Now you need to assign waypoints in order to stay on schedule.

In step 5, divide your current annual income by 12 to find your average monthly commission income. Now take the adjusted income goal calculated earlier and, in step 6 subtract your current annual income to determine the additional monthly income needed.

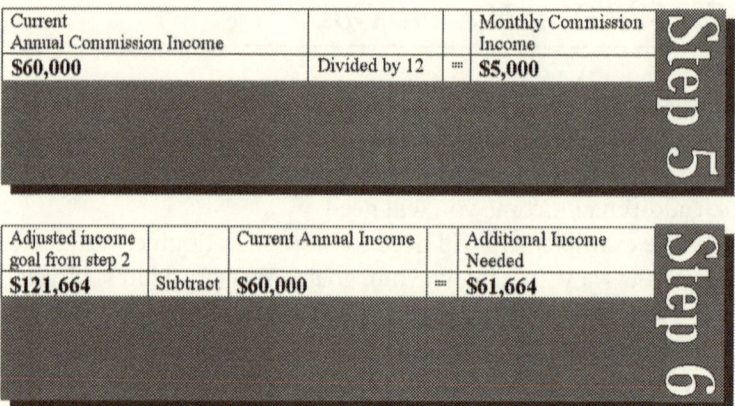

Current Annual Commission Income			Monthly Commission Income	
$60,000	Divided by 12	=	**$5,000**	Step 5

Adjusted income goal from step 2		Current Annual Income	Additional Income Needed	
$121,664	Subtract	**$60,000**	= **$61,664**	Step 6

Notice that we are using the adjusted income goal, but we are not using the adjusted current income. This may seem like an oversight, but it is not. The adjusted current income allows for account attrition, business you will lose due to circumstances beyond your control. This is business you'll have to plan on replacing while you grow your overall business activity.

Now, in step 7 take the additional annual income needed from earlier in this chapter and divide it by 12 months to determine the additional monthly income needed. If this was based upon a five-year goal such as I used in the example, divide this number by 60 months in step 8 to determine how much commission growth you'll need per month.

Additional Annual Income Needed			Monthly Commission Income Needed	
$61,664	Divided by 12	=	**$5,139**	Step 7

Additional Monthly Income Needed			Monthly Commission Growth Needed	
$5,139	Divided by 60	=	**$86**	Step 8

Use these numbers in step 9 to create a time line so that you can document and track your progress toward your goal.

Year 1

	JAN	FEB	MAR	APR	MAY	JUN	JUL	AUG	SEP	OCT	NOV	DEC
Current Monthly Income	$5,000	$5,086	$5,172	$5,258	$5,344	$5,430	$5,516	$5,602	$5,688	$5,774	$5,860	$5,946
Projected Monthly Growth	$86	$86	$86	$86	$86	$86	$86	$86	$86	$86	$86	$86
Projected Monthly Income	$5,086	$5,172	$5,258	$5,344	$5,430	$5,516	$5,602	$5,688	$5,774	$5,860	$5,946	$6,032

Year 2

	JAN	FEB	MAR	APR	MAY	JUN	JUL	AUG	SEP	OCT	NOV	DEC
Current Monthly Income	$6,032	$6,118	$6,204	$6,290	$6,376	$6,462	$6,548	$6,634	$6,720	$6,806	$6,892	$6,978
Projected Monthly Growth	$86	$86	$86	$86	$86	$86	$86	$86	$86	$86	$86	$86
Projected Monthly Income	$6,118	$6,204	$6,290	$6,376	$6,462	$6,548	$6,634	$6,720	$6,806	$6,892	$6,978	$7,064

Year 3

	JAN	FEB	MAR	APR	MAY	JUN	JUL	AUG	SEP	OCT	NOV	DEC
Current Monthly Income	$7,064	$7,150	$7,236	$7,322	$7,408	$7,494	$7,580	$7,666	$7,752	$7,838	$7,924	$8,010
Projected Monthly Growth	$86	$86	$86	$86	$86	$86	$86	$86	$86	$86	$86	$86
Projected Monthly Income	$7,150	$7,236	$7,322	$7,408	$7,494	$7,580	$7,666	$7,752	$7,838	$7,924	$8,010	$8,096

Year 4

	JAN	FEB	MAR	APR	MAY	JUN	JUL	AUG	SEP	OCT	NOV	DEC
Current Monthly Income	$8,096	$8,182	$8,268	$8,354	$8,440	$8,526	$8,612	$8,698	$8,784	$8,870	$8,956	$9,042
Projected Monthly Growth	$86	$86	$86	$86	$86	$86	$86	$86	$86	$86	$86	$86
Projected Monthly Income	$8,182	$8,268	$8,354	$8,440	$8,526	$8,612	$8,698	$8,784	$8,870	$8,956	$9,042	$9,128

Year 5

	JAN	FEB	MAR	APR	MAY	JUN	JUL	AUG	SEP	OCT	NOV	DEC
Current Monthly Income	$9,128	$9,214	$9,300	$9,386	$9,472	$9,558	$9,644	$9,730	$9,816	$9,902	$9,988	$10,074
Projected Monthly Growth	$86	$86	$86	$86	$86	$86	$86	$86	$86	$86	$86	$86
Projected Monthly Income	$9,214	$9,300	$9,386	$9,472	$9,558	$9,644	$9,730	$9,816	$9,902	$9,988	$10,074	$10,160

Step 9

In this example, the $61,664 needed in additional income may have seemed enormous, perhaps unattainable and unrealistic. When broken down, it's less than $86 in commission income growth per month. Use this method to achieve any goal that you set your mind to. I used it to lose 70 pounds. 70 pounds is a lot! Since I set an objective to lose the weight over a one-year period, I only needed to lose six pounds per month or less than a pound and a half per week. Chances are, you will reach or exceed you initial objectives, and that will supply the motivation to forge ahead. Before you know it you'll be there, probably ahead of schedule!

What Is Your Average Account Worth?

Take your current annual commission income and divide it by the total number of accounts to determine the average commission income generated per account.

The fact that it's an average implies that several accounts generate more than this amount and some generate less. We aren't deciding what to do with any of them yet; we're simply building awareness. What the average tells you is this: If you continue to develop your client base with the same general strategy that got you to where you are now, you can predict what you'll have to do to reach a higher income level.

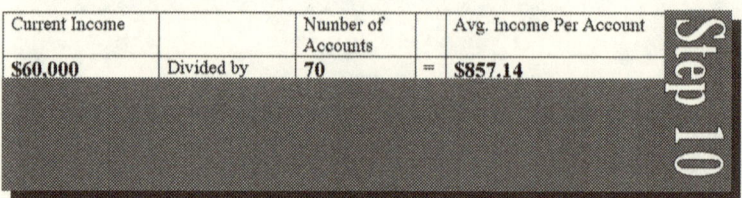

Current Income		Number of Accounts		Avg. Income Per Account	
$60,000	Divided by	70	=	$857.14	Step 10

How Many Additional Accounts Will You Need?

In step 4, you determined how much additional income you'll need to reach your financial goals. In step 10, you calculated what your average account contributes in terms of commission income. In this step, you'll calculate how many additional accounts you'll need. Simply divide your additional income needed from step 4 by the average income per account from step 10.

If, as in the above example, you currently maintain 70 accounts and you need 88 more to reach your financial goals, that means you'll have 158 total accounts to maintain! How vulnerable do you think you'll be trying to keep that many customers happy? Now are you depressed?

Additional Income Needed		Average Income Per Account		Number of Additional Accounts Needed	
$75,237	Divided by	$857.14	=	88	Step 11

How Much Time Will You Need for Existing Business?

Take your total number of active accounts and determine the number of hours spent each month maintaining that business. Be sure to include time traveling, waiting, entertaining, collecting, order processing, and any other activity directly related to maintaining your accounts. Divide that number by four weeks to determine, on average, how many hours per week you're working to maintain your existing business. Finally divide the hours per week by the total number of accounts to see how many hours per week on average you need to maintain each account.

Total hours per month spent with existing accounts			Approximate number of hours per week spent with existing accounts		Number of accounts	Hours per Week per account needed to maintain existing business		Step 12
120	Divided by 4 weeks	=	30	Divided by	70	=	.43	

If, as in the above example, you spend an average of 120 hours per month or 30 hours per week actively maintaining your existing business, you're averaging just under a half hour per account per week. This number may seem low until you think about it. There are probably accounts that you spend considerably more than a half hour per week working with. There may be accounts that you don't see every week.

How Much Time Will You Need for Your Financial Goals?

Take your number of existing accounts and add the number of additional accounts you'll need from step 11 to determine how many total accounts you will be maintaining. This assumes that you will continue to add the same general mix of business. That's the total number of accounts you'll have to maintain. Take that total number of accounts, and multiply it by the hours per week per account in the last column of the chart in step 12. That is how many hours per week you will be working maintaining business once you've signed all these accounts.

Number of Existing Accounts		Number of Additional Accounts You Need		Total Number of Accounts to Maintain to Reach Income Goal		Hours per Week Per Account: Existing business		Hours You Will Spend per week Maintaining Business once Signed (not including all non-selling activities)	Step 13
70	+	88	=	158	X	.43	=	68	

Now how depressed are you?

Hopefully you are depressed enough to take action. Look back and review your list of goals. How many of your goals are marked with a T indicating that they require time? Study the list and approximate how many hours you will be able to work and still have time to achieve all of your time sensitive goals. The message should be clear. You don't need more accounts; you need better accounts. This awareness leads you to examine your hourly wage.

What Is Your Hourly Wage?

If, as in the above examples, you're earning approximately $ 60,000 per year in commission, that's approximately $1,200 per week. ($60,000 divided by 50 weeks allowing for 2 weeks vacation). If you're working an average of 50 hours per week including all non-selling, commuting, and administrative time, you're earning $24 per hour, your current hourly wage calculated in step 14.

Your hourly wage goal is calculated in much the same way. As illustrated in step 15, if your personal income goal is $121,664 and you intend to accomplish that in a 40-hour workweek, your hourly wage goal would be just over $60 per hour.

Complete the previous calculation tables for your specific circumstances so that you have a clear picture of where you're headed. Only then can you get specific about how you're going to get there.

Annual income from commission			Weekly commission income		Hours worked per Week		Your current hourly wage	
$60,000	Divided by 50	=	$1,200	Divided by	50	=	$24.00 per hr	Step 14

Annual commission income goal			Weekly commission goal		Hours worked per Week		Your hourly wage Goal	
$121,664	Divided by 50 weeks	=	$2,433	Divided by	40	=	$60.83 per hr	Step 15

Notice from your list of goals that nearly every item that is marked with a $ or a T is directly impacted by your choice of career. Many of us put in long hours in hopes of achieving those financial goals marked with a $, therein providing a greater standard of living. All too often, however, we find that striving for a greater standard of living erodes the overall quality of life since the long hours reduce the time available for the goals marked with a T.

The trick as we dive into the action steps in the "Selling by the Numbers" process is to achieve greater income while working the same or fewer hours. It's simple math. If you can earn the same income working half the number of hours, or if you can earn twice the income working the same number of hours, you'll double your hourly wage. Only then do you have the power to decide whether you want to savor the newly found time and work on achieving those goals with a T or if you want to use the newly found time to work more in order to achieve the $ goals. Through controlling your hourly wage comes the power to steer your life where you want it to go. That's the real beauty of a career in commissioned outside sales. You determine your hourly wage!

5

Putting the Plan into Action

"The U.S. Constitution does not guarantee happiness, only the pursuit of it. You have to catch up with it yourself."
—Benjamin Franklin

Evaluating Your Current Customer Base

When was the last time you examined each customer to determine how much money they put in your pocket and how much time they require for that income? If you had to think about the answer, it's been too long. More importantly, if you have done it, when is the last time you compared that number against your overall target? If you're not doing this regularly, how do you determine whether or not a new prospect is worth your time? How do you determine if an existing customer is worth your time? If you've ever needed an attorney, you know that they have a set hourly rate. Whether they're talking to you on the phone, meeting in an office, writing a letter on your behalf, or appearing in court, they charge that hourly rate. If you want to just sit in their office and shoot the breeze, they don't mind. At a couple hundred dollars per hour, they'll give you as much time as you want. You must start thinking like an attorney. You, too, are a professional.

Once you have these two numbers, take a look at each of your accounts to see which of your current customers are paying you what you're worth and which are not. Be sure to include all the time that you spend with each customer such as drive time, paperwork time, time on the telephone, time meeting with support people regarding the account, and so forth. We will dive into this process in greater detail in the section that follows. The results may astound you.

Create Your Zones

The quickest way to raise your hourly wage is to cut out wasted time. For most road warriors, windshield time is their largest block of wasted time. Can you do a better job of grouping your accounts into a route so that you can visit more of them in less time? Every organization I have worked with has a select group of "star" salespeople. They drive from one corner of their territory to the other responding to customer urgencies. They get frazzled and frustrated, but somehow believe that they put in a fair day's work for a fair day's pay. Why don't they just break them into areas and see everyone that's in a given area at the same time? On paper it seems simple enough, just "plan your work and work your plan!" In reality, it's not quite that simple. Customers today can be very demanding. You must take an objective look at your daily activity and ask yourself, "Are you running your territory, or is your territory running you?"

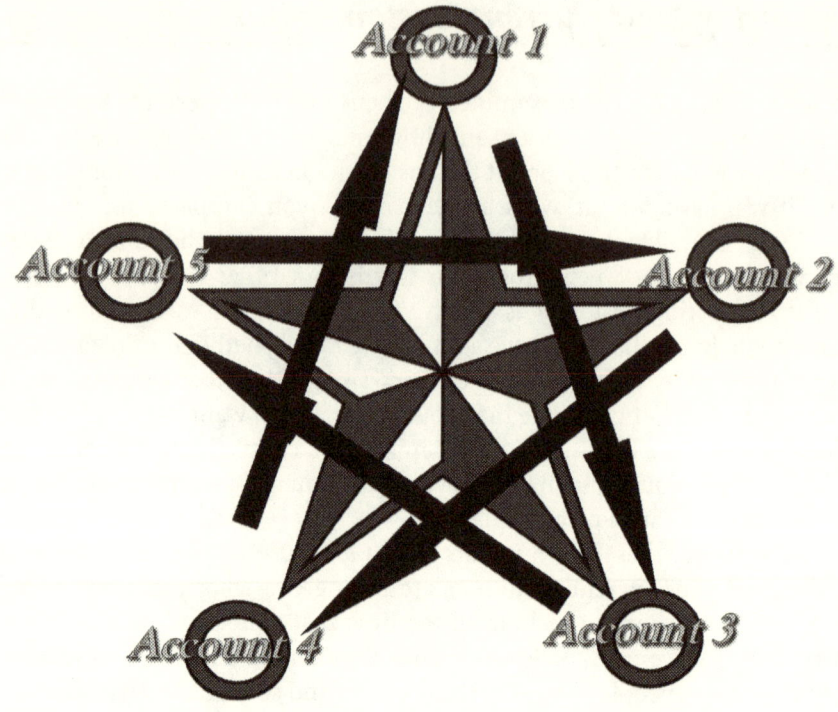

If this is happening to you, there are really only two reasons, and you must critically evaluate your activity to determine which one it is.

➤ You failed to make a plan.
➤ You failed to follow the plan that you made.

I'm guessing that it's a combination of the two. At some point, you were frustrated enough to make some kind of plan. Within a few days, your most demanding customer or customers had some crisis causing you to vary from the plan. Before long, the plan was little more than a pipe dream so you were forced to scrap it. Go through this exercise in futility a couple of times, and you no longer waste time planning. You feel as if it's out of your control.

Notice, both alternative causes involve failure. This is why most won't acknowledge it. If you play the part of the victim and swear that it's your customer's fault and not yours, you will fail to reach your goals. You will convince yourself that the solution is in your customer's power to control, not yours. Gee whiz, how motivating is that? Either way you look at it, you're a failure! Oh but there's a tremendous difference! The difference is taking control of your life by taking responsibility for your failure. If your customer is the cause, only he or she can fix it. Since you can't make them do anything, you're doomed. When you acknowledge that you are the cause, you can fix that, and I'll help show you how!

Remember that the time spent to maintain includes driving or *windshield* time. The only way to reduce this is to cluster your calls. Unlike the star salesperson, an organized salesperson eliminates as much non-productive time as possible. Few activities are as unproductive as sitting in traffic or rolling down a highway. Rookie salespeople often feel like as long as they're in the car on the way to see a customer they're working and that as long as they're working they're doing their job. WRONG! Success in selling is about productivity not activity. The most effective approach I've seen used by the most organized salespeople is a form of a cloverleaf. They divide their marketing area into four or more zones.

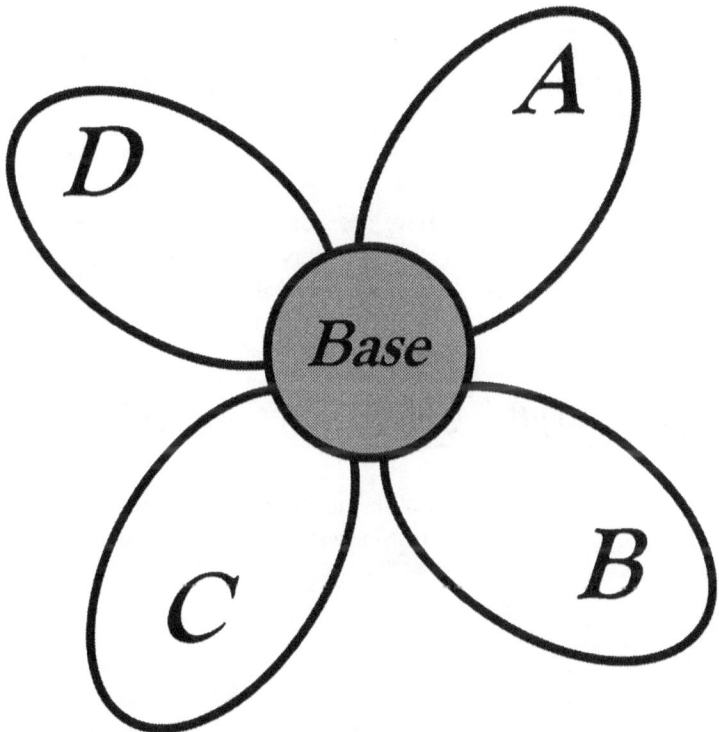

On any given period, the salesperson will be working one of these zones. If you have a localized territory, one where you're home every night, you divide your territory into four zones, one zone for each day of the week leaving one day for wiggle room. Each day is spent in one of the zones. If you cover a larger territory requiring overnights, a cloverleaf approach still works, but the zones are individual weeks, not days. There are several tremendous benefits to this approach.

➤ It virtually eliminates wasted windshield time.

➤ It instantly illuminates where you need additional business. It may turn out that one or more of the zones is chock full of existing business, so prospecting activity on those days will be minimal. Other zones may be weak. Prospecting may consume most of your time on those days.

➤ Since the zones are contiguous, it's not as difficult to squeeze in an urgency on the edge of one zone if something comes up in a neighboring zone that you absolutely cannot get out of doing. This allows you to squeeze it in and get back to your planned activity so you stay on track with your goals.

Get a map large enough to display all of your current active customers. Grab a marker and start marking the location of each account on the map. If you have a computer, mapping software and the knowledge to use it, you can do this electronically. When you're finished, take a long hard look at the map. Some kind of cloverleaf possibilities will appear. It will change over time, so don't worry whether or not you have it exactly right. If traffic is an issue, try highlighting roads where you're likely to have problems during rush hour. Revisit the map often and consider how you might modify your routes to miss some traffic congestion.

A Place for Everything and Everything in Its Place

Once you've laid out your accounts on the map and identified zones, create a file folder for each zone. A ringed binder with tabbed dividers also works well.

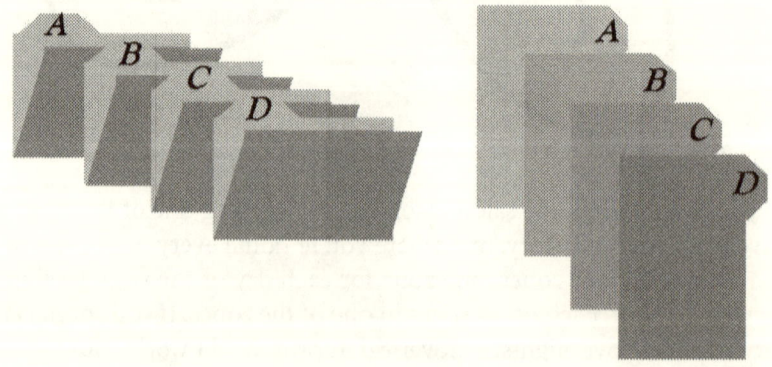

Create the following three overview lists for each folder.
1. Active Customers by Zone
2. Prospects by Zone
3. Suspects by Zone

Samples are provided on the following pages. Blank worksheets are included at the back of the book.

Once you have all of your customers and prospects listed, you'll want to create a record card for each. Examples of the cards are as follows. The front page should be a quick overview of important account facts. The back page is for call notes. If additional space is needed, you can use notebook paper and staple it to the card.

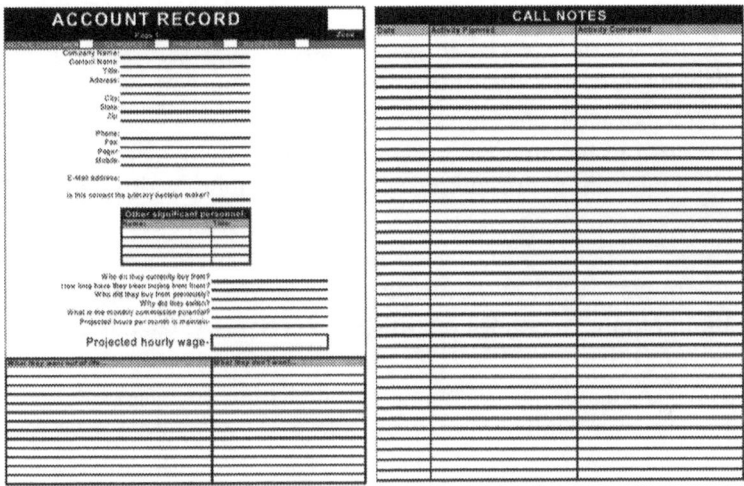

We'll categorize potential business as being one of three things. Each is a conquest, a prospect, or a suspect. Suspects are any potential business that you know very little about. All potential new business starts as a suspect. Once you've learned a little bit about them, they become either rejects or prospects. In general, your prospects are those potential customers that have made it past the first screen (Do they fit your needs?) and are in the process of being pulled through the second screen (Do you fit their needs?). Each call on these prospects should result in some kind of advance. You don't want to let too much time go between visits even though consistency and persistence are not yet critical deciding factors. Conquests are those accounts that are a good fit for you, and you are a good fit for them. All that's left is to figure out how to sign them. More precise description of each is addressed later during the Prospecting System in chapter 7. These record cards will be your roadmap for each account helping you keep track of where you are in the process, what you've accomplished, and what still needs to be accomplished.

If you use these cards correctly, you will increase your hourly wage. Here's how you use them:

➢ Throughout each day, you're likely to think of things you want to talk to these people about. When you do, pull out that person's card and jot a note. That way, if your phone rings, or you pull up at another customer's to make a sales call, the thought doesn't fade away. Trying to remember everything can be maddening. Writing all the thoughts down somewhere and then trying to find them can be even more frustrating. When you have a card for each, you can put the note right into their record and get back to whatever you were doing.

➢ Keep track of times when your customer is busy. If you find yourself driving out to see a customer and can't because he or she is too busy, you're reducing your hourly wage. You need to ask what time of day is best or call for an appointment. If your customer likes to waste your time by talking and talking, you might choose a time that is a little busier for them so that they are more inclined to get to the point and move on. Before you do anything rash, be aware of where you are in the process, a skill we'll discuss later in the book. If you're trying to build rapport or smoke out hidden objectives, small talk is not a waste of your time.

➢ Have an agenda for EVERY call! Decidedly few activities will erode your hourly wage faster than stopping into your customers and/or prospects with nothing important to discuss or accomplish. Stopping in just because you were "in the neighborhood" is a really bad system. It sends a message to your prospect that you don't plan your time. Why should they respect your time if you don't? It says loud and clear that it's okay if they don't have time for you because you have very little worthwhile to talk about, and you're not inconvenienced since you are just passing through the area. It sends a message that they must not be very important since you didn't make a special trip. Each call should be designed to result in an advance. Whether you're handling a problem, proposing a new product or service, or something else, have a reason for every visit. If it's a customer you haven't seen for a while and you just want to check in to be certain that everything is okay, that's still an agenda. Don't just stop in to ask, "How's everything?" Be specific. Have reports documenting the business you've done so far. Examine the product or service you sold them. Talk to others in the organization to see how well the product or service is working for them.

➤ You accelerate the process of signing new business by making sure that you secure an advance on each call. If you don't record what you want to talk about or what you did talk about, you wind up duplicating some effort. Duplication erodes hourly wage. By reviewing the card prior to each sales call you can get an overview of the history. Perhaps the greatest value to the cards is their ability to capture and utilize stray thoughts. When you're in sales, you spend a lot of time thinking. You never know when a great idea will hit you regarding how you might approach or impact any specific account. It's not enough to just have some place to quickly write it down. That stray note may not be present right before your sales call when you really need it. If you forget it on your next call but remember it later, it's too late. Failure to retrieve the information in time for the very next call is sure to prolong the solicitation process. If you don't have some record to look back and see your progress, you really have no idea how quickly or how slowly the process is moving. At the beginning of each week, you'll want to pull out the cards and plan your week. Take a hard look at each account, and determine if each call is truly required. When scheduling your sales calls, review the notes on the cards. If nothing needs to be discussed, consider if you really need to make that visit. Sales call notes on prospects should be like milestones. Selling is a journey. You'll want to see if you've been making progress on each visit. Without some tracking mechanism, salespeople tend to fall into a routine stopping by because they happened to be "in the neighborhood." Again this wastes both your and your customer's time.

Each time you leave a customer or important prospect, take a few minutes to think about what might be worth addressing at the next visit. Look at your monthly overview to see when the next visit is scheduled, and make some notes on their record card. Whenever you think of something that you want to cover on the next visit, go to the card and write it down. There are several contact management software products you can use if you have a laptop computer. If you need to travel by airplane, you might seriously consider using one since files are tough to carry around. Paper or electronic, you need to have some place to gather and sort this information. Now you can look at all the cards for each zone and start hard scheduling.

Hard Scheduling

You're going to need a month-at-a glance calendar. There are several computer based planning programs that also work well. If you're not a techy, a simple monthly planning book works fine.

Hard scheduling is for your foundation customers, your project customers, and your conquests. These terms will be defined in detail in subsequent chapters. These are people that you want to make absolutely certain are seen with frequency and consistency. With foundation customers, there is usually something important to talk about. With project customers, you may be exploring growth opportunities and add-on sales in addition to general business issues.

Start by choosing one flex-day per week for wiggle room. This is the day you leave open for urgencies. When a holiday falls in a given week, that day can be your flex-day. Hard scheduling is done one of two ways and I'll address them individually.

Small territory without overnights:

With a small territory, a four-week rotation works best. Since you have four zones, assign a zone to one day each of four weeks. If a customer or conquest is worth two calls per month, schedule them into every other week on their day. If the next customer on the list is worth one call per month, schedule them every four weeks. If a larger customer is worth four calls per month, schedule them into every week, and so on.

	MONDAY	TUESDAY	WEDNESDAY	THURSDAY	FRIDAY
Week 1	ABC Company ☺			Open	Diversified Products?
	A	B	C		D
Week 2			Modern Industries	Open	
	A	B	C		D
Week 3	ABC Company ☺			Open	
	A	B	C		D
Week 4		Western supply ☺		Open	
	A	B	C		D

If any account scheduled is providing you with an hourly wage in excess of your long-term goal, identify it in your schedule with a smile ☺. Labeling your calendar in this way will allow you to quickly identify who must be seen come hell or high water and who you can miss if you start to run out of time. Any time you're able to free up, no matter how little it is, improves your hourly wage!

Large Territory with Overnights

With a large territory, a three-month rotation may work better. Monday or Friday make good wiggle room days for obvious reasons. Then you assign a zone to each week. Scheduling consistency when you cover a large territory is particularly challenging and especially important. Contiguous zones really pay off when you have accounts that need more than one visit per month. If an important account is on the edge of two zones, you can schedule a visit on the front edge of one route and also on the tail end of another without disrupting your plan.

	MONDAY	TUESDAY	WEDNESDAY	THURSDAY	FRIDAY
Week 1	ABC Company ☹	Diversified Products??			Open
Week 2			Modern Industries		Open
Week 3					Open
Week 4		Western supply ☺			Open

Soft Scheduling

Soft Scheduling is for your trouble accounts and your prospects. Trouble accounts are the active accounts that you can most easily afford to lose because they are not generating enough to meet your average hourly wage. Trouble accounts are written in with a frown ☹. They will be the first calls you don't make if you find yourself running out of time. Less time with them accomplishes two things. Your hourly wage increases (same income less time), plus you're spending time with higher value prospects that, once signed, are more valuable than your trouble accounts. There is an exception to this rule. If any of your trouble accounts have more potential that you're just not getting, you do not want to de-emphasize them, quite the contrary. You should think of them as two separate entities. First, the time justified for the amount of business you are getting. Anything beyond that should be considered potential new business and treated like a prospect.

Standby List

Standby is more than the list of suspects. Most salespeople treat a list of suspects as a "wherever, whenever, no big deal if I don't get to them" list. That's not what I'm talking about. If you've ever traveled standby on a commercial airline, you know what I mean by standby. A standby passenger is eagerly waiting to get onto an otherwise sold-out flight. It's good for the airline since a certain number of guaranteed passengers are likely to cancel leaving empty seats on the plane. It's good for the standby passenger because he or she might get a seat on an otherwise sold-out flight. In order for this to work, the standby passenger must be waiting at the gate with all necessary papers and be ready to jump on at the last minute. If a seat does not open up, he or she goes to the next flight out and waits there.

That's what a standby list is for. You don't schedule these. In any given day some calls will take a little longer than expected and some will go more quickly. Anytime that you find yourself ahead of schedule, it's helpful to have a quick reference of suspects that you can work into an open spot in the schedule.

The Paredo Principle

The Paredo Principle is more widely known as the 80/20 rule. The Paredo Principle states that 80 percent of your business comes from 20 percent of your customers. I've had the opportunity to analyze the customer base for hundreds of salespeople, and I am still amazed at how accurate the rule is. Check your customer base and see for yourself.

To do this, start with a list of active customers ranked from high to low. Then draw a line under 20 percent of your customers.

Then add up how much you're earning from that top 20 percent and divide it by the total. If you're like most salespeople, that percentage will be remarkably close to 80 percent!

Here's why you do this. Customer intimacy comes from having a smaller customer base. The purpose of this exercise is to illustrate which customers you can live without. When planning your time, you must keep the top 20 percent satisfied: They make up the lion's share of your income. In

	A: ACTIVE CUSTOMERS	B: Commission generated per month
Account Name		
1 ABC Industries	$	1,880.00
2 Consolidated	$	1,034.00
3 Action Products	$	624.00
4 Johnson Supply	$	420.00
5 Modern Corp	$	214.00
6 Favorite Stores	$	135.00
7 Advanced	$	125.00
8 Miller & Miller	$	100.00
9 Parkway Products	$	90.00
10 Anderson and Sons	$	72.00
11 Main Street	$	68.00
12 City of Springfield	$	57.00
13 Heritage	$	43.00
14 Lakepoint	$	41.00
15 Quality	$	32.00
16 Cardinal Service and Supply	$	23.00
17 Reed's	$	20.00
18 American	$	16.00
19 Federated	$	14.00
20 NewAge products	$	12.00
21		
22		
23		
24		
25		
26		
27		
28		
29		
30		
TOTALS	$	5,020.00

order to grow your business, you must find the time for your prospecting efforts. With an awareness of your own 80/20 status, you'll know right away whom you can afford to take the time away from. You will find prospects that can provide you with enough business to replace three or four of your smallest customers, yet require the same or less time. It becomes a migration. You constantly review your bottom 80 percent while looking for individual prospects that can replace several of your less lucrative accounts.

Over time, your smallest customers will be larger than your medium customers are right now. As this happens, you continue to apply the Paredo Principle focusing on replacing the smallest of these large accounts. There's a bonus! Even though you took time away from the small accounts to do your prospecting, they don't all just go away. The ones that remain become the icing on the cake. Even though you have replaced the business, many of the small ones continue to buy. When this happens, your hourly wage explodes!

The Paredo Principle not only helps focus your efforts, it helps keep your company infrastructure focused as well. Few things are as frustrating for your service or operations department than trying to remember the idiosyncrasies of hundreds of individual small accounts that only purchase on an occasional basis. When you have a smaller number of accounts that purchase more frequently, your support people get accustomed to their needs and are more likely to keep them happy.

The more effective your support staff is at keeping your customers happy, the less time you have to spend struggling to keep their business. With more business in less time, the end result is obvious. Up goes your hourly wage!

6

Tetris Time Management

"The meeting of preparedness with opportunity generates the offspring we call luck."
—Anthony Robbins

Time Management Defined
Your time is your life.

No book on selling would be complete without covering time management. Did you ever stop and wonder, "What, exactly is time?" You could talk about hours and minutes, but those are measurements. I've heard someone describe time as a sequence of events, one after the other. Some define time in terms of a period or interval. Okay, if they say so. I've been told that time flies when you're having fun, time waits for no man, time is of the essence, there's no time like the present, and time is money. I still can't quite get my arms around it. Is time finite or infinite? I think there was time before I was born, though I wasn't here to know for sure. I can assume there will be time after I die, though I won't be here to confirm it. I am certain that I personally have only a fixed amount of time on this planet. The older I get, the shorter that time seems to be, and the faster it seems to go. What becomes particularly depressing is the realization that so much time has passed, and you're not very far from where you started.

So then what is time management? Can you manage time? You can manage staffs of people. If you run a business, you can add people or subtract them. You can tell them what to do or not do. You can manage money. You can spend it or you can save it. You can earn more or you can choose to stop earning it. But time, we eventually realize, won't be managed. You can't get more and you can't tell it what to do. Time just marches on saying, "You're not the boss of me!" Time is the ultimate equal opportunity provider. Each day, we're given 24 hours and we have to decide what to do with them. There will never be any surprises. Inflation won't give us more or less than the allotted 24 hours. No competitor has more, none has less.

Time management is badly misunderstood. Far too many people believe that effective time management means filling up every second with something to do. If they have too much free time, they take on projects, which we will refer to later in this chapter as *chores*. If free time is becoming scarce, they turn away projects. If their calendar is full, they feel content. If their calendar is too full, they feel stressed. If it's not full enough, they feel anxious. Effective time management is not about staying busy. Real, meaningful time management is about your goals. You must spend most of your time working toward those things that are important to you. When you over-schedule your time, you will miss opportunities to move toward your life goals. If you never identify your goals, you'll plow through life achieving whatever comes along. Someday, it will catch up with you.

Triage
"If everything's under control, you're just not going fast enough!"—Mario Andretti

Champions don't complete everything on their to-do lists. Real champions are effective time managers because they start with their goals and work their activity around them. Since mediocre performers never define their goals, they tend to resist time management. If you're not passionate about where you're going, how do you allocate such a precious resource by managing every activity along the way? Time management is not just about *how* it's about *why*. When an activity is scheduled into an open slot, you must be certain why it needs to be done. Time management does NOT mean taking everything you currently have to do and fitting it into some kind of time slot. Not only doesn't it work, it works against you! Effective time management requires intimate knowledge of the concept of *triage*.

Triage is, according to *Webster's*:

A. A process for sorting injured people into groups based on their need for or likely benefit from immediate medical treatment. Triage is used in hospital emergency rooms, on battlefields, and at disaster sites when limited medical resources must be allocated.

B. A system used to allocate a scarce commodity, such as food (or time), only to those capable of deriving the greatest benefit from it.

C. A process in which things are ranked in terms of importance or priority.

"For millions of Americans, each week becomes a stressful triage between work and home that leaves them feeling guilty, exhausted and angry"—Jill Smolowe

Triage means examining all the activities that you might do and determining which ones are part of the solution and which are not. All too often, activities get prioritized based on urgency instead of importance. We do the urgent ones first. The problem is that the urgencies just keep on coming. You feel like you gave a fair day's work for a fair day's pay, but you finish each week no closer to your goals. You must focus on what's important, not what's urgent.

Some of your competitors are bigger, some faster, some more experienced, some better capitalized, and some better educated, but there is one thing that you all have exactly the same amount of, **time**. Michael Jordan may be a hero for scoring 44 points, but if it took him seven games to do it, he wouldn't be much of a hero. In sales, you may think you're a hero for making three sales, but if it took four years to make them, you probably won't earn bragging rights, at least not in most industries (There are a few exceptions in large ticket sales, but you get the idea). Success is measured both in terms of results and time.

I probably haven't told you much that you didn't already know. But are you doing it consistently? If not, why aren't you? This stuff is pretty simple. Probably because the fact that it's simple does not mean that it's easy. Motivation and energy run like waves in the ocean. You will have highs and lows. Through some periods, your highs will be moderate, as will be your lows. In more turbulent times, the lows may seem unbearable, but the highs that follow may be tremendous. A successful selling career will include a system for minimizing the lows and maximizing the highs.

That's easy to say in theory, but what does it mean in practice? First and foremost, you must clearly define your goals. Then, if you're going to achieve them, you must make the very best use of your time. You must prioritize. Before you can juggle priorities, you have to know how to prioritize. Everyone thinks that they know how to prioritize only to find at the end of the day, it just didn't happen. It's harder than it seems.

You must start with the discipline to list everything that needs to be done. If you're doing this in your head instead of doing it on paper, you're not really doing it at all. Every activity you list will have two vital components, time and importance. Regarding time, each activity either has to do with today, right here and now, or it has to do with the future. With regard to importance, it either is important or it is not. Think of your to-do items being stacked onto one of four trays. The first two trays deal with right here and right now, they are your emergencies and your urgencies. The last two trays have to do with the future. They are your goals and your chores.

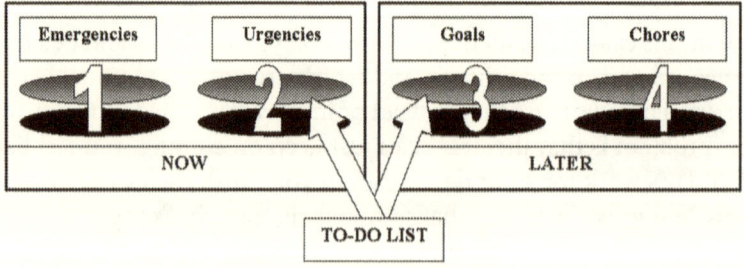

Tray one, emergencies, will be done right here, right now for obvious reasons. As an example, you slip and fall, cutting yourself badly. Seeking medical attention is urgent since you only have a certain amount of blood to lose. It's important if you would like to be around to see tomorrow. You don't need to prioritize these items. They will prioritize themselves. Everything else gets pushed back on the list. At the other end is tray four, your chores. These activities are not terribly urgent, nor are they very important. Take, for example, organizing a closet. Unless you just can't find what you're looking for, it doesn't seem urgent. Since you can close the door to keep it out of view, it doesn't seem all that important. Like emergencies, chores also tend to prioritize themselves. They never make the list, and they don't get done unless there is nothing else to do. All remaining activities now compete for the fixed number of hours remaining in each day.

Then there are the activities that fall onto the two remaining trays in the center called urgencies and goals, and this is where most salespeople fall down. Goals are activities that are important to you, but are not urgent. When you're seventeen years old, saving for retirement may be an important goal, but it sure doesn't seem very urgent. Urgencies are, as the name implies, urgent but they are not important. When you're sitting watching TV and the phone rings, it seems urgent (most people hang up after six or seven rings) but it may be unimportant (it might be a telemarketer). Overly simplistic examples like these seem painfully clear. Categorizing all your goals (important, but not urgent) and urgencies (urgent but not important) may not be so simple.

What Does Important Mean?

If you did not take the goal setting exercise in chapter 4 seriously, go back and do it. All sales champions have taken the time to clearly define their goals. All of them! Whatever time you saved by not completing the exercise will be wasted struggling with this issue on a daily basis. Which of your daily activities are most important will become crystal clear once you have properly identified ALL of your goals in life. What's left is to evaluate whether or not the activities you're facing contribute to those goals. We are all motivated by getting something that we want or losing something that we don't want. This is a key component of time management. Remember that, for most people, emergencies and chores tend to prioritize themselves and they don't belong on a to-do list. When a champion looks at the two middle trays with all of the to-do items, he or she looks at the goals first, then chooses activities consistent with the goals. Since the mediocre majority rarely takes the time to define goals, when they have a few minutes of free time and look at their to-do list, all they have is urgencies and chores. When they complete the urgencies, they do chores. Do you plan time with your family, time for exercise, time to stop and smell the roses, time to read a good book, and time to unwind and de-stress? You might if you've identified these things as being important during your goal setting (soul searching) exercise.

The *Selling by the Numbers* process takes this to the next level into the rarified air of peak performance. You start with a comprehensive list of goals. You mathematically calculate what is needed to achieve those goals. Then, finally, you translate those activities into an action plan with milestones and waypoints to keep you on track. You no longer talk in terms of *if* you achieve your goals. Instead, you find yourself talking in terms of what they are and when you will achieve them.

If you are not goal oriented, your focus will always be on the first two trays that represent the here and now and the fourth tray once you're caught up. Champions focus almost exclusively on tray number three, which is in the future. Tray four chores are also in the future, but not because they're something you want that you have to wait for; rather because you don't want them and you've procrastinated them away. That's a critical distinction. Champions work on tray three activities because they want to achieve something. Others work on tray four activities because they want to get them over with. Motivation is all about getting what you want (goals) and/or avoiding what you don't want (chores). When the mediocre are unmotivated, it's because they have successfully procrastinated the chores well into the future and have no goals. There is no motivation to be found in trays one or two. You don't go to them. They come to you! And there is surely no motivation to be found in tray four. These are activities you typically dread. Motivation will always be found exclusively in tray three.

A Real To-Do List

After you've developed your list of goals, you must develop the discipline to write things down. When you think of something you can do that might help you achieve one of your goals, write it down. If it later looks silly, you can cross it off. If you have clearly laid out your goals and started writing in your to-do list those activities that will help you achieve those goals, you're well on your way.

The to-do list is just a temporary holding cell, someplace quick to write down ideas. At the beginning of each day, look at your list and start inserting the activities into your schedule. As a vague to-do list, both the importance and the urgency get lost. You will convince yourself that you will get to them sooner or later. When they're inserted into a schedule, they inherit a deadline and their likelihood of getting done increases dramatically. Each day, review the previous day's list. If the activity is still necessary, move it to another day.

Be realistic. If the day looks too busy to complete everything on your list, move the activity to another day. If it's no longer important, cross it off and forget about it.

We're assuming that there is enough time in each day to accomplish everything that you scheduled. Herein lies another pronounced difference between top performers and their lower performing peers. People who haven't mastered prioritizing tend to do one of two things.

➤ They list anything and everything that they can think of and start working the list from top to bottom hoping to complete them all. What they don't complete is moved to the next open slot in their schedule. Urgencies tend to get done, importance tends be lost or overlooked. Unless you've taken the time to determine what's important, you will have a difficult time choosing which items on your list are most critical. Instead of moving forward with purpose toward your goals, you wander aimlessly through the abyss. If you don't know where you're going, you probably won't get there.

➤ They stop adding anything to the list since they don't think they're going to finish what is already on it. If they haven't listed their goals in life, much of what gets done was urgent, but may not have been important. Many important activities never made the list for fear that they weren't going to get done.

In a high-performing lifestyle, lots of things just won't get done! If that makes you feel like a failure, it's because you did not take the time to list your goals. Failing to complete every activity that comes your way is not the same as failing to reach your goal. Not only is it okay to leave some to-do items undone, it's essential! The more activities you have listed that might contribute to your goals, the more you'll have to choose from to determine which will provide the greatest impact. The better you become at listing all possible activities, then filtering out the ones with the lowest potential contribution, the more progress you'll make each day toward your goals. List everything you think of. The primary purpose of a to-do list is avoiding task saturation. Throughout each day, you'll think of many things that could or should be done. If you try to remember them all, several will inevitably get overlooked. If you force yourself to remember everything, you won't be able to operate at peak effectiveness. Your mind works much like a computer. A computer has two primary types of memory, your RAM and your disk drive. RAM or random access memory is for programs that are open and running so that you can move quickly through your work. Once a project is finished, you save it to a disk drive for long-term storage. If you spend much time on a computer, you know that when you have too many programs up and running at once, it slows down dramatically. It may even lock up. When this happens, you need to close a few programs and free up that RAM for the more important programs. Your mind works the same way. If you find yourself slowing down or locking up, write a few of your less critical tasks on your to-do list so that you can focus on the more critical tasks at hand.

When reviewing the daily items not done, think hard about rescheduling them. Compare what's left on the list to what did get done that day. For so many people, the things that got done were more urgent than the things that didn't get done, regardless of whether or not they were important. You must develop the discipline to say no to urgent tasks when they compete with your goals. This is the dilemma described in this chapter. When you say no to urgent tasks, they don't get rescheduled. If they were urgent, it's probably too late. If they were urgent and important, they would have prioritized themselves, and they would have been done. Your important tasks got done instead, and you moved closer to one or more of your goals. If you're failing to plan, you're planning to fail.

Playing the "Slots"

There is a video game named Tetris® where a series of different shaped blocks descend from the top of the screen. The object is to move and twist these blocks as they drop so that, by the time they hit the bottom, they fit into your open spaces. The game is over when a block tries to descend and has nowhere to go because other blocks have reached the top. If you start the game and do nothing, assorted shaped blocks fall haphazardly and quickly reach the top leaving lots of open spaces. That's what reactive time management is like. If you just take every activity as it comes, you will eventually run out of time and leave a lot of time unutilized.

Manufacturing leaders have historically taken a hard look at this process. Their objective is to identify all the activities that must take place from start to finish (these are the different shaped blocks) and figure out how to fit them together so that there is no wasted time (open spaces). It works well for manufacturing process because the goal is clear as are the individual tangible activities required. Since this was largely an industrialized nation for the entire twentieth century, the same approach was taken toward all business related time management, including sales.

But it doesn't work for sales. The activities are not concrete and tangible. To succeed in selling you must persuade people. When you're dealing with people, you're dealing with emotions. The concept of fully utilizing every moment still applies. How you will fill each space is very different. In manufacturing, it is critical that you perform the same activity in exactly the same way every time. Try that in sales, and you're not a salesperson; you're a robot. Robots cannot persuade people to buy. Unlike manufacturing, some activities just won't get done. Some you will do because they were worth a try, and you would never have known until you threw it out there.

Like Tetris®, your schedule only has a fixed number of open slots. As you build your customer base, your demands and your opportunities start filling up your slots. If you aren't careful, you'll wind up having wasted or empty slots. With respect to maintaining existing business, the process more closely resembles the manufacturing mindset. You determine who needs to be seen and how much time they require and slot them in, making the best possible use of the time.

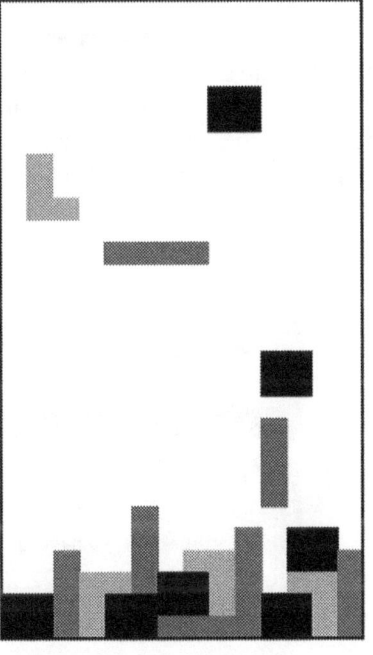

Tetris® Time Management means you start to view every open space in your calendar as the once in a lifetime opportunity that it really is. We all have 24 hours in a day, no more and no less. You can't lose them, you can't create them, and you won't fill every slot. If you fill every time slot, you're working as hard as you possibly can. This approach can be devastating to a career in selling. The object of the game is not to work as hard as you can. Rather it's to make the most effective use of any slot that you fill! Open slots are a good thing! If you have open slots in your schedule, you can do planning, prospecting, fire fighting, entertaining, or whatever you want to do *without* disrupting critical selling activities. If your organizational goal is to fill every slot, you will constantly be juggling priorities, and important activities will be bumped by urgencies.

Each account is like a series of Tetris® blocks that need to be fitted into your schedule. The size of the block shows how much commission they represent to you. The shape of the block represents how much time they require.

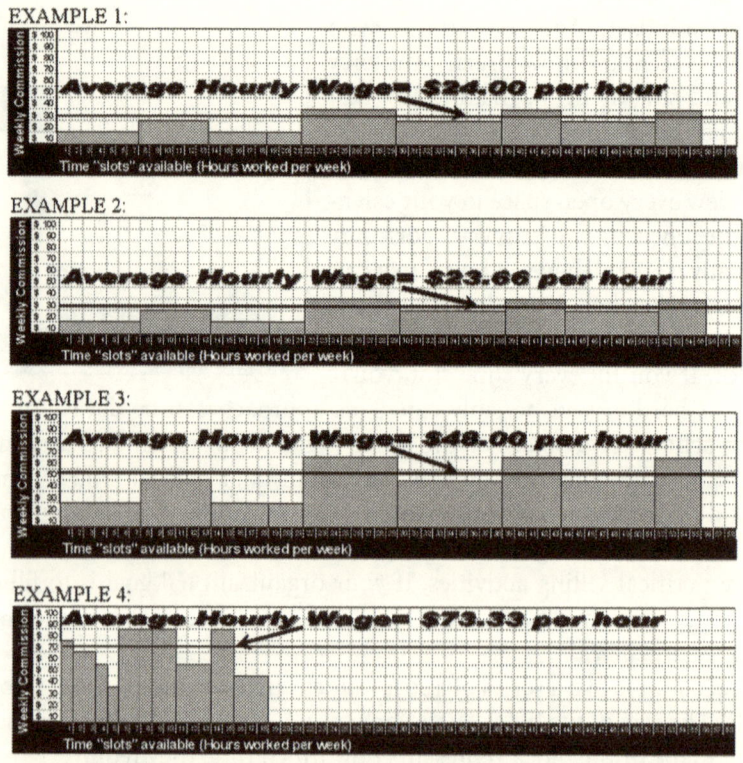

If, as in the above example, each block represents $10 in commission income, the blocks on the left represent an account that will allow you to earn $40 in commission for each hour spent ($40 per hour). The blocks on the right represent an account that will generate the same $40 commission income, but requires a four-hour investment in time ($10 per hour). The following four charts illustrate the impact of hourly wage per account awareness.

EXAMPLE 1:

Average Hourly Wage= $24.00 per hour

EXAMPLE 2:

Average Hourly Wage= $23.66 per hour

EXAMPLE 3:

Average Hourly Wage= $48.00 per hour

EXAMPLE 4:

Average Hourly Wage= $73.33 per hour

In example 1, if you have nine accounts generating a total of $1,320 per week in commission requiring a total of 55 hours to maintain, you're working for approximately $24 per hour.

The Three Ways to Increase Your Commission Income

1. **Work more hours.** This won't improve your hourly wage; it may actually reduce it. You'll simply trade time for money. If you land one more similar account and make no other changes, you'll earn more commission, but you'll work additional hours maintaining it. The net effect is depicted below in example 2. In example 2, your additional account boosted your weekly income by $100 but required 5 additional hours to maintain for a net of $20 per hour. Since this new account generates an hourly wage less than your previous average, your overall average is now only $23.66 per hour.
2. **Have bigger accounts.** In example 3, you have the same number of accounts taking the same amount of time, only each account is larger and generates more commission income. If each account from example 2 were twice as large and required the same investment in time, your hourly wage would be $48 or twice as high. This is a much better plan than just adding more accounts.
3. **Spend less time on each account.** In example 4, the same nine accounts from example 1 are slotted into 18 hours instead of the previous 55 hours (We turned the Tetris blocks up on end). If you can pull this off, your average hourly wage just skyrocketed to $73.33. As a special bonus, time slots are now free to prospect for additional business, and you'll now have the free time to handle more business once it's signed!

To put the theory into practice, complete the following chart for your existing customers. In column A, list your top 30 customers. In column B list the monthly commission you earn from each account. In column C, estimate how much time you spend maintaining each account. In column D, divide the commission (Column B) by the time (Column C) to reveal the hourly wage earned from each individual account.

A: ACTIVE CUSTOMERS Account Name	B: Commission generated per month	C: Hours spent per month maintaining	D: Hourly Wage B/C
1			
2			
3			
4			
5			
6			
7			
8			
9			
10			
11			
12			
13			
14			
15			
16			
17			
18			
19			
20			
21			
22			
23			
24			
25			
26			
27			
28			
29			
30			
TOTALS			

Understand and Categorize Your Current Business.

"Before you travel the world digging for diamonds check first to see if there are any in your own back yard."—Earl Nightingale

The accounts that are paying you an hourly wage at or above your goal are your **foundation accounts**. They are not part of the problem; they are part of the solution. If any of them seem vulnerable, tighten up your relationship with them. These are accounts that you really can't afford to lose.

The next group of accounts that you'll want to focus on consists of those accounts that are generating an hourly wage above your current average, but below your goal. These **project accounts** are neither part of the problem nor part of the solution. Carefully examine how much time you spend with these accounts, and then ask yourself these key questions.

➤ Do you stop by just to say hello with nothing important to talk about?
➤ Do you spend a lot of time cooling your heels waiting to see the buyer?
➤ Do you drive far to see them only to find that they had to leave the office?
➤ Are they outside your normal marketing area without any other accounts in the area to justify the trip?

If any of these are the case, you may be able to plan better and reduce the time you spend each month maintaining them. Then examine your penetration at these accounts. If you are only getting part of the business, an increase in your penetration into this account might raise them over the hump so that they become a foundation account.

The toughest ones to deal with fall into the last group. These are the accounts that currently generate an hourly wage below your current average. Often, these are the smaller accounts that you signed early in your career when any piece of business was welcome. They're the ones that "brought you to the dance." They may be accounts where you quickly bonded with they buyer because you had something in common with them. They may have been a referral. The buyer may be someone who left one company that you dealt with and now works for another smaller company. Most frequently, these are the accounts that you just plain enjoy working with so you spend more time with them. Whatever the case, these **trouble accounts** are not part of the solution; they are part of the problem! Left alone, they will cause you to hit the glass ceiling and keep you from ever reaching your goals and dreams. It is imperative that you ask the same battery of questions listed for your project accounts. Your goal is not to throw your accounts away, rather to find a way to get your existing account base in line with your goals. If you can't find a way to get them up to your hourly wage goal, commit to replacing them. Of course I'm not suggesting that you walk in and say "I don't want to do business with you anymore; you're not worthy." I am implying that you gradually spend less time with them so that commissions earned justify the time spent.

When you do this, you'll start to find yourself with free time. This free time can be spent prospecting for more and better foundation accounts. With hourly wage awareness, you'll also know which accounts you can afford to steal time from in order to chase better accounts. Your account list will gradually migrate from smaller, more time consuming accounts to larger, more lucrative accounts. With the awareness of the hourly wage contribution made by each of your existing accounts comes a fresh approach to prospecting. When asked, "What makes a good prospect?" your response, simply put, will include how much commission you can expect to earn from this account AND how much of your time the account will demand?

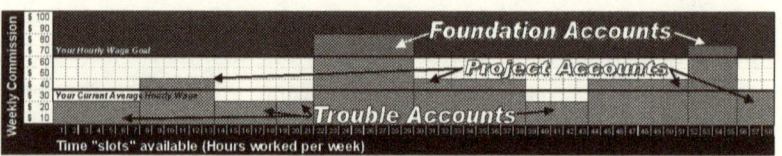

This approach will fine-tune your customer base and your prospect list so that it is aligned with your greatest opportunities for long-term prosperity. It does not mean that you should abandon your existing accounts in order to chase the "whales." Rather, it's a gradual migration from smaller, less lucrative accounts to larger more lucrative accounts. It's like pruning a tree. You have to continually trim off the small less important branches freeing up nutrients and sunlight needed by the primary branches. Having bigger accounts means having more sales, right? Duh! Of course it does. But does it mean a higher hourly wage? Not necessarily. Large accounts do, however, tend to offer the greatest opportunity for a high hourly wage for several reasons.

➢ Large accounts depend on more than just you, they require infrastructure. Much of the time required to maintain the business is not your time.
➢ These people tend to be busier. Stopping by to shoot the breeze is a waste of your time and theirs.
➢ They are more likely to work by appointment, so you'll waste less time.
➢ There are economies of scale. If a medium account needs one sales call per week, it's unlikely that an account five times as large will require a call every day.

So why don't we all just go out and land the larger accounts? There are several reasons.

➢ Many salespeople just don't know how. Selling to a large account is a very different sale than selling to a smaller account.
➢ Some salespeople are intimidated by larger accounts.
➢ There just don't seem to be enough hours in a day. Large accounts take longer to land. It doesn't make sense to take time away from the existing accounts in order to chase the large ones. Like they say, "A bird in the hand is worth two in the bush." You've already bought into my earlier

discussion about quality of life and hours worked. You have no idea how you would find the time to identify, understand, and land any large accounts let alone handle them once they're on board.

➤ Some salespeople claim to shy away from large accounts on purpose, afraid to let any large account make up more than a small portion of their business. They don't want "too many eggs in one basket." That's narrow-minded thinking. Done properly, selling by the numbers does not mean getting rid of all your small accounts to have one big account. Instead of bending your future to accommodate your client base, you'll be learning how to fit your clients into your plan.

Whatever the reasons, you can overcome them. Most new salespeople feel more comfortable with smaller, less sophisticated accounts. They're easier. They typically want to land as many of these as they can to start putting some numbers on the board. They also need to start landing some accounts to stay positive and motivated. The problem is, once signed, they tend to dominate your time leaving very little time for a concerted effort on larger more elusive accounts. Large accounts are tougher. Calling on them often causes inexperienced salespeople embarrassment, frustration or demoralization, so they slide back into their comfort zone calling on smaller accounts.

You can make as good a living on a large base of small accounts as you can with a small base of large accounts as long as you carefully manage your time. On the upside, with a lot of small accounts, no single account can have a devastating impact on your income. On the downside, you tend to lose a critical piece of the selling puzzle, customer intimacy. To visualize what's meant by customer intimacy, imagine having a party. If your party has 300 guests, there's a real chance that some of them are not having fun and you don't even know it. They may get bored or irritated and leave. They may have felt ignored in the big crowd and their feelings might be hurt. If a few in the crowd start to get a little rowdy, your time and attention will not be spent with the people who are most important to you, rather it will be spent with the people who are likely to do the most damage. You may be so busy with the large group that you didn't even notice your friends leaving.

Now picture a small dinner party with a dozen or so close friends. You'll be able to spend quality time with each. You may be able to bring a few of them together adding a new dynamic to the group. You can stay close enough to each to make sure that everyone is having a good time. This is a key difference. With a large group you are less likely to focus on the ones who are *not* having fun. Conversely, with a small group, you will be keenly aware of each participant and whether or not they are enjoying the party.

Once You Choose the Track, Stay on Track

Consider how long a typical sales call *should* take. While some will take longer than others, it's crucial to have a time frame in mind. When you go into each call with a time frame in mind, you tend to get to the point more quickly. When you do this deliberately and consciously, several things happen.

> ➤ Your prospects will become easier to see since they know you'll get right to the point and not waste their time.
> ➤ You tend to stay focused on the issues at hand. With an open time slot, conversations tend to get sidetracked. If you get too far off course, it can be tough to get back.
> ➤ You obviously stand a better change of getting more done in a day.

So how long should a sales call take? Pick a number, any number. Only after you pick a number do you become consciously aware of how much time you really need and how much time you waste.

Force the Discipline

This system works. It's not the only one that does, but it's the best one. I've worked with many salespeople searching for that perfect time management tool. I've seen salespeople go from Franklin planners to Daytimers to PDAs to laptops to homegrown systems and more all in search of that perfect organization system. They try them hoping that each will force the discipline to get more organized. I've done it myself. It's a bit like the weekend golfer buying new clubs hoping it will make him or her a better golfer. I've learned the hard way that you can't buy a golf game and you can't buy time management skills. Effective time management comes from committing to learn and practice the fundamentals first, then fine-tuning them. Your approach to organization is the network of roads connecting your current position to your destination in life. The books, calendars, forms, folders and programs are simply vehicles.

Forcing the discipline is, for many, very difficult. With discipline come both the ability and the necessity to occasionally say no. You must take the time to schedule your customers and your prospects in such a way that it maximizes your time and efficiency. If you do so, and one of your demanding customers calls later in the day with his or her crisis du jour, how quick are you to abandon your plan and respond? When you do, you commit several serious errors. The very first time you do it, that customer will know that his or her time is more valuable than yours. Do it once and that customer is likely to expect it every time. Like any bad habit, the longer they've been allowed to do it to you, the harder it will be to break them of it. The calls from the demanding customer often start with a casual question like "Hey, what are you doing?" If you answer with something cavalier like "Oh not much, what's up?" you're sunk. Now you can't say that you're too busy, you just told him or her that you're not doing much. You might not have meant it, but you said it, and that's all that matters! It's just as bad to say something negative like "I'm having one of those days!" That sends a message that you normally engage in crisis management, so one more crisis from an important customer should not make a tremendous difference.

Instead, try rehearsing something positive and enthusiastic like, "I've got a great day lined up for today, lots of exciting things going on. How can I help you?" Or you might say, "Super busy, all good stuff. What's up?" It may sound a bit corny but it works. Often, if the customer is accustomed to dominating your time, he or she might simply say, "I've got a problem; can you stop by?" Once you hear the request, don't be negative or aloof. Try responding with something like, "I'm not in your area until next Wednesday, but why don't you tell me what's up and let me see if I can handle some of this over the phone so you don't have to wait that long." You may be genuinely surprised at how many issues you can address without disrupting your schedule. Until you force that discipline, there's no real point to developing a hard plan. Doing so will only lead to frustration. Once you start to get it down, you start controlling your time. Once you're deep into a *Selling By The Numbers* system, this response will become intrinsic. You'll send a message that your time is very important because it will be. Every moment counts.

Dependability, consistency and follow-up are very important. Together, they equal integrity. If you say you'll be there every three or four weeks, schedule it into your calendar. If you don't, your integrity and dependability will be suspect. If this is not a conquest, ask if you can stop by and visit with them from time to time just to be there in case they need anything. Don't be specific on the time frame unless you plan to put it into the schedule and commit to it. I've landed numerous customers due solely to diligent follow-up.

My favorite example is a large fleet in the southwest. My competitor was the industry leader, and this was a high profile fleet. Since I worked for a second-tier company, many prospects in this league did not take my company or me seriously. My first sales call was in the spring. The prospect told me that they were happy with their current supplier and saw no reason to change (I'm guessing you've never heard that; it's called a put-off objection). I could tell he was simply blowing me off since he was doing business with the industry's premier supplier and he didn't take me seriously. I thanked him for his time and promised to stop by from time to time just to see if there were any changes. When I stopped by a few weeks later, I received a similar response only this time with a little more feeling. Something like, "There's no point in your stopping by. I'll call you if anything changes." By the way, if you don't already know it, they don't call. That's just a prospect's way of saying that they see little value in what you offer.

Now I don't mind being told that my capabilities don't fit someone's needs, but I can't walk away until we've had a chance to explore their needs and my capabilities thoroughly enough to see if they do or do not fit. The tough part can be getting your prospect to take the time to explore with you. There is a fine line between being persistent and being pushy, only you typically don't know that you've crossed the line until it's too late. If you'll remember, the first objection from the last paragraph was a put-off. He was hoping I would go away without his having to be rude to me. The second was a more spirited put-off. There is no point to keeping this up. You can't win. If you turn it into a contest between your pushing and your prospect pushing back, it will probably escalate until you both lose.

So do you simply back off? I don't think so. I told him, "I think there's a good chance that I bring something to the table that is of value for your fleet. I can see that this is a busy time for you and that, of all the problems and challenges you have to wrestle, this is currently not one of them. I'm a long-term player. If this is not a good time for you, I surely don't want to become a pest. Is there a time anywhere in the future that your schedule might free up even a few minutes to sit down and learn about each other to see if there is anything I might be able to do to help you achieve your objectives?" To the casual observer, I'm inviting the prospect to blow me off. And he did. He responded with, "Why don't you call me later in the summer?" I asked, "mid-August sometime?" He said, "Great!" He thought he just got rid of me since 99 out of 100 will never follow up. I went to my calendar and wrote this fleet into my plan for August 15.

Between this conversation and the meeting, I did a lot of research. I asked other fleets in the area about them. I used the Internet. I watched in the trade press. When I found articles relative to his business, I would send him a copy with a quick note that read, "I thought you'd find this interesting. See you mid-August." First thing in the morning, August 15, I called for my appointment. Do you think he agreed to meet with me? Of course he did. By then, he could tell that I was different from the other salespeople he'd dealt with, including the salesperson from his existing supplier. Most of all, he could tell that I was committed to the process and to the relationship. In business, there will always be problems and challenges. Commitment is often the sole difference between success and failure. My prospect knew that I was committed to success and that I was committed to having him be part of the success. I signed him as a new customer.

These are relationship strategies more than selling strategies. Selling is about relationships. Rookies often view selling as if they had a little black book with the names and numbers of a hundred or so potential partners. They go through the list every so often and call out of the blue to see who might be interested. Because the prospects only hear from the salesperson sporadically, they tend to feel like prey, and the salesperson is the predator. The ones who say yes are probably the ones who aren't tied up with someone else. They are the worst ones that nobody wants. They're available for the following reason. They jump quickly from relationship to relationship, so they're constantly between mates and they are not loyal to whomever they're with. In any case, hoping to use this method to find a solid fulfilling long-term relationship is pretty ineffective.

Instead of the little black book approach, lock your sights on the ones that you really want, the ones that everyone wishes they had. Zero in on the ones that will provide you with the most fulfilling long-term relationship, then focus all of your attention on them. Show them that you are committed to winning them over, whatever it takes. Show them that you care and that you are a long-term player. It takes longer to be sure. The payoff, however, is immeasurable. Instead of spending time replacing customers, you're spending the time adding more customers. That's how you build a successful career in sales.

7

Prospecting System

"You miss 100% of the shots you don't take."
—Wayne Gretzky

Determining Your Prospecting Needs

Obviously, if you're planning to grow your income, you need to grow your business, which will inevitably include prospecting for more. Before you hit the streets looking to sign something, you need a crystal clear picture of what you're looking for. If you sign new business that's inconsistent with your goals, you'll actually move farther away from your objective. In the previous chapters, you performed a series of calculations to define where you are right now and how far you have to go. You were encouraged to take a hard look at those customers that provided you with an hourly wage below your goal. Remember that the calculations in the previous chapter were based upon the complexion of your existing business as it stands today.

The first step in improving your hourly wage was to use time management skills to accommodate the same business with less time. That alone will improve your hourly wage. The next step was to examine your penetration of each account to see if you can boost your income within your current customer base. Once you've fine-tuned your existing customer base and your use of time, redo the calculations. Only then can you know exactly what you'll need in terms of additional business.

New business has three purposes.

➤ To replace any account that generates an hourly wage substantially below your goal.

➤ To provide the additional income needed to achieve your five-year income goal.

➤ To replace the business you will inevitably lose to attrition.

Prioritizing Prospects

Size:

Are hot prospects the ones with the most potential business? Keep in mind that the one everybody wants will have many competitors vying for the business. In addition, your competitors are likely to have their best salesperson assigned to the largest accounts. They may even assign a team of people. You will not win this customer with a casual occasional visit. It will require a full-scale assault and lots of planning. Don't even get started if there's a chance you can't give it the effort it deserves! If you get started, then fade away for a while, your credibility will be shot, and all time invested prior to that point would be wasted. That wasted time kills your hourly wage.

Once signed, your large prospect will be very demanding. When evaluating your potential income from the account, be realistic about the demands the account will have on your time, and do the math. Compare the hourly wage you'll earn on the account against your current hourly wage and your long-term hourly wage goal. There's no faster way to hit an income ceiling than to sign a tremendously large and demanding account that requires more time than it deserves in terms of personal income generated. Visit with your manager and ask how much infrastructure and support you can depend on to absorb the more mundane, time consuming activities that will be required. Be certain you and your company are fully prepared to handle this account in the event they say yes. If you get the business and can't handle it, you'll lose it fast and with it, all your credibility! You'll also have wasted a lot of time that could have been spent on more valuable activities. If the numbers just don't work, as hard as it is to do, you may consider letting your competitor have this one and keeping digging. At the very least, that's one competitor that will be too busy to solicit business from your customers or prospects.

Difficulty:

The buyer that makes you feel most comfortable is often the customer you really don't want. The buyer that is the toughest to get close to will be a better customer. Most salespeople who come across the tough prospect get hurt feelings, decide that they don't even want to do business with this "jerk," and they don't go back. Since it's human nature to avoid people who seem abrasive, your competitors are probably avoiding them as well. The incumbent supplier, therefore, enjoys a fairly solid position. Conversely, if your prospect always has a few minutes for you, he or she probably has a few minutes for all of your competitors. The nice, kind, buyer who doesn't challenge you probably doesn't challenge your competitor either. Once you sign this customer, they will continue to allow your competition to get their ear and woo them. Your position will always be tentative.

The prospect that's the easiest to get is also the easiest to lose. It may be the one nobody wants! They may be so demanding and unreasonable that your competitors would be glad to lose them. They may be so price sensitive that no one wants them. They may not pay their bills promptly. If timely payment is an issue, you're likely to spend many hours just trying to collect for what's already sold. In addition, every time they go on the past-due list, you'll probably be forced to suspend deliveries pushing that business to competitors. Talk about lowering your hourly wage. These accounts will prevent you from building your territory. Let your competitor have them. It'll keep him or her out of your way for a while. It's far too difficult building a territory if you're spending all your time replacing lost business. Landing new accounts will not help you grow your business if you're merely replacing business that you've lost. The answer lies, not in working harder to land even more business, but in being very selective about the accounts you're working to sign. The more poach-resistant your existing accounts are, the more long-term impact your new account solicitation will have.

Unlike shoppers, your loyal customers generally won't continuously beat you up for a lower price. Even when they do, it's usually sufficient to come close to but not beat the lowest price. Shoppers also have this nagging tendency to keep you on shaky ground so that you don't take them for granted. As such, you wind up spending an inordinate amount of time fending off attacks from your competition. The deadly combination of more time and reduced pricing destroys your hourly wage!

Quantity vs. Quality:

Most salespeople don't consciously prioritize prospects at all. Rather, they make as many calls as they can on as many prospects as they come across hoping that one or more will be open to listen. These salespeople depend on a haphazard blend of serendipity and tenacity. Even referring to this activity as *prospecting* is a stretch. It's really nothing more than taking a survey. You're going door-to-door asking, "Do you want to change suppliers?" You do this in hopes that, if you're in front of enough of them, you'll be there when one of them wants to switch. This approach is driven by a fear of rejection. Weak salespeople do it because it's easy and non-threatening. You aren't really selling at all so there is nothing for the person to object to. Does this approach work? Yes, unfortunately it does to a limited extent. That's why so many salespeople do it. Some accounts might get worn down with persistence until they say yes, and it's marginally better than not making the calls at all. At least the chances are now greater than zero. Like the other non-strategic approaches, they'll eventually cause you to hit an income ceiling and a pathetic hourly wage.

There are other problems with this approach. You may stop in to see an account once or twice per year hoping that you'll be around when and if they plan to switch. Another competitor may have been stopping in more frequently. When they are ready to switch, what makes you so sure that they'll switch to you. An effective sales process reveals to you AND YOUR PROSPECT what is really needed. Often, it's the period of discovery that crystallizes your prospect's understanding of the problem, as well as providing a vision of the potential solutions. Handled properly, the solutions that your prospect envisions will be consistent with your unique strengths. When you go door-to-door taking a survey, your competitor may have opened them up to the possibility of switching and they may have already guided the decision toward factors that were consistent with their strengths, not yours. Trying to change your prospect's concept at this point is extremely difficult and rarely works.

Depending on your industry, you may think that there are tons of good prospects out there. As you filter through your suspects, you will find that there may only be a small number of prospects that are capable of providing the hourly wage you need. You must be able to quickly sort through them, determine their *value* and move on, focusing on the most lucrative prospects before your competitor does. Leave the remaining, less lucrative accounts for your competition. The best thing you can do is to fill up their time with these less valuable customers. The busier they are with those accounts, the less time they'll have to go after your high value prospects. As with the great gold rush, imagine a group of people heading west prospecting for gold. Let everyone else start digging into every nook and cranny along the way in hopes of finding some tiny piece of gold. While they're busy, you move forward toward the richest potential opportunities and stake your claim. Some of the richest strikes took place high in the mountains in the most remote reaches of the western wilderness. Simply put, if it were easy, everyone would be there doing it.

From another perspective, I'm reminded of a cable TV show on the Learning Channel named "Clean Sweep." The crew of this show visits people helping them clear out rooms that are knee-deep in mounds of clutter. Most of these people just won't part with anything because they just might need it someday or it has some sentimental value. Unfortunately, everything is so buried that they don't use or enjoy any of it, often forget they even have it, and can't find it if or when they really need it. Whether you're talking about prospects or household belongings, clutter is clutter. If it's out of sight, it is out of mind.

In order to move forward, you must decide what's important and clear out the clutter. Choose your best opportunities and overcome call reluctance. It's easier than you think. Effective immediately, once you've determined you best opportunities, walk into them determined to find a way that your product or service can make their life better in some way. Don't walk in with the purpose of selling them something. If someone were in need and you knew that you could help, would you be reluctant to offer? Conversely, if that person had something that you want, would you be reluctant to ask for it knowing that they might say, "No" and resent your asking? When you deeply understand the implications of those two questions, you'll realize that a spirit of help is the only way to overcome call reluctance. Always remember, selling is something that you do FOR your customers, not something that you do TO them.

Categorizing Prospects

Suspects To Prospects:

Effective prospecting is the act of scooping up and sifting through the tons of *suspects* in order to find a few decent *prospects*. Think of the 49ers—not the football team but the masses of people in the 1800s venturing west prospecting for gold. While digging, an awful lot of rock gets thrown away into a pile. In selling, this act of sifting through those suspects is called *qualifying*.

This initial qualification should be short and sweet. You need to determine several things.

> ➤ Are they credit worthy?
> ➤ How much can they buy, and how much can you earn with them?
> ➤ How much time will they require?
> ➤ Using the answers to those two questions, determine how it compares to your current hourly wage and your hourly wage goal. If it's more than you're making now, the account is worth pursuing, even it's less than your ultimate goal.

When sorting through suspects, your primary decision should be "Are they right for me?"

Conquests:

Those making it through the initial qualification are only those accounts that look promising. You don't yet know whether or not they will help you reach your goals. You must now explore each of your prospects more thoroughly. Since the list is now smaller and more manageable, you should be taking a hard look at the current status and next step every week. As you uncover critical information about each prospect, you should be comparing their wants and needs against you and your company's specific package of value. Over the next few visits, a select few will stand out as being a particularly strong fit. These, we call your conquests!

As you elevate a prospect to a conquest, you've already determined that he or she might be right for you. What's left to determine is whether or not you're right for them.

By the time a potential account has been elevated to the status of conquest, you must be committed to aggressive persistent consistent solicitation. You should be saying to yourself, "This one is mine! I can be a better supplier to this account, and nothing or no one is going to stop me from getting an opportunity to prove it to them!"

If, at any time, you are not advancing on each and every call, it is no longer a conquest; it's really just a prospect. Conquests are only those accounts where you are deeply engaged in a contest with your competition and are committed to making them your customer.

Cinderella Story

In the fairy tale Cinderella recall that the quality of the glass slipper meant very little. The final decision of who gets to marry the prince came down to whether or not the shoe fit. Your single most important account selection criterion lies in a determination of how well your strengths fit the wants and needs of your potential customer. Earlier in the book, we explored methods for determining what your prospect wants and needs. Once you do, you must compare that to what you do best. Be honest and realistic. If your prospect's current supplier is a better match with what they want, shake hands and let them go. If you are better capable of meeting those wants and needs, you owe it to your prospect to tell them. Often, even if they choose to stay with their current supplier, they will "raise the bar" once you leave the office. In the months that follow, your prospect may become increasingly critical and demanding of their current supplier. You may not even be aware that it's taking place. In some cases, it takes place subconsciously. Your prospect may become more demanding and not even realize it themselves!

Like the Cinderella story, if you want to go from rags to riches it's not good enough to be *better* you must be a better FIT. You must match their specific wants and needs better than your competitor. In business-speak, the term for the fit is differentiation. How effective are you at describing precisely how and why you are different from each of your competitors? If your answer is simply, "We're the best," you are missing the point, and you will not succeed. If any of your competitors are successful at all, there is something they do well. Fortunately, all prospects are not created equal. The first key to success is in knowing why you and your organization are uniquely superior, then finding those prospects that need that flavor. Your organization and each of your competitors have a unique personality. Likewise, each potential customer has it's own personality. Matching them is the secret to effective, long-term business relationships. Trying to force them together or matching them up hoping they'll grow together doesn't work very well. You're left trying to find business to replace the lost customers while your customers are left trying to find a replacement supplier.

What is a good differentiator?

If your prospect is focused solely on price and your competitors have more competitive pricing, you'll spend a lot of time landing an account that you may lose very quickly. The customer that comes on price generally goes on price. If you are, in fact, the low price leader but offer limited service, you'll want to focus on those that are willing to live without service in order to get the lower price. When you're "Selling by the Numbers," you must compare your strengths and your shortcomings specific to *each* competitor. The following chart illustrates how you need to think about it.

Package of Value Comparison

How likely are we to get AND TO KEEP the business?

Specific to each prospect, for a specific competitor, what is most important to your prospect?

Rate from 1 to 10 how well you and your competitor perform on each item (10=best)					
		US		THEM	
POV Component	Weight	Rating	Score	Rating	Score
Acquisition price	10	1	10	5	50
Total cost of ownership	9	1	9	5	45
Quality	8	2	16	4	32
Service	7	2	14	4	28
Salesman Expertise	6	3	18	3	18
Brand preference	5	3	15	3	15
Selection	4	4	16	2	8
Delivery	3	4	12	2	6
Warranty	2	5	10	1	2
Billing	1	5	5	1	1
Total			125		205

Each prospect will require his or her supplier to provide specific products and services. In a chart like the one above, list each component of the package of value (POV) required by your prospect. List them from the top to the bottom in order of importance to your prospect. If you don't know your prospect well enough to list these components, you're putting the cart before the horse.

Once you've listed them in order of importance, assign a weight from 10 to 1 for each item. 10 is for the component most important to your prospect, 1 is the least important. The four columns to the right are used to score your ability to meet their requirements compared to your competitor. Rate yourself and your competitor on each component. Then multiply the weight of each component by the rating for each component to score your value on each component. Repeat this process for your competitor. When finished, add up the scores and see who appears to be a better supplier. The higher score wins. If you do this exercise at least once, you'll start to develop an understanding of the process used to evaluate suppliers. If you're really comfortable with it, sit down with your prospect and go through the exercise together. You might learn something as you and your prospect grow closer together. This exercise will reveal several things:

➤ Do you really know what's most important to your prospect? This is the quest that will drive your call agenda. This is why you keep prospect records.

➤ Do you know everything that's of value to your prospect? A decision to change suppliers never comes down to a single criterion. Even if you don't have a marked advantage in their most important criteria, you may be significantly stronger at other critical components.

➤ Remember that a decision to buy or not buy will always come down to the four factors described earlier. These components are the bricks that tip the scales. Your prospect will decide to buy if they're convinced that they will get more of something they want or avoid more things that they don't want. They'll abandon their current supplier if they think that, by staying with them, they'll get more of something they don't want or lose more things they want. If it's going to work, each of the components you list must be individual factors that your prospect has confirmed he or she wants or needs.

➤ After completing the exercise a few times, you will begin to see trends. You will develop an awareness of your company's differentiators that consistently give your an edge. You'll also start to notice certain characteristics that make a prospect good for you.

Success is about differences. When you know how your company is different from your competitor and how each prospect is different from the next, you can determine who your best fitting prospects will be.

Size Matters:

There are all kinds of things important to your prospects. There are a few biggies that will help or hurt you with nearly every prospect. The biggies help you sort quickly through the first selection so that you can focus on a smaller number of prospects that have a better chance of fitting your capabilities. One of the clearest differentiators is your capability relative to the size of the account. Landing and servicing a large account is very different from landing and servicing a small account. Companies that supply large accounts seem to be better positioned to handle them and not as effective with smaller accounts. While large companies may offer consistency across large geographical regions, smaller companies tend to excel in terms of flexibility and customer intimacy. Likewise, salespeople tend to have a comfort zone relative to the size of the account. To categorize accounts and prospects, it's helpful to group them by size. Accounts tend to fall into one of four categories.

➤ Whales: It takes a community to land a whale. Whales are the giant accounts that everyone in the industry knows. Landing a whale requires large investments in capital equipment. It also requires large staffs of people, each with his or her own duties and responsibility. With regard to whaling, rogue independent thinking employees are not part of the solution, they are part of the problem. Whale accounts are your highly visible national industry leaders. A national department store chain is an example of a whale. Even the very best salesperson will not be effective landing or servicing these accounts without a great deal of support from his or her company's infrastructure. A single whale may take a long time and a lot of people to land. Once done, the entire community will eat for a long time. To be successful landing a whale you must be able to coordinate the efforts of numerous disciplines within your organization.

➤ Muskies: Often called the "fish of 1000 casts (or an experienced guide)." A muskie is a sport fish. While proper equipment is important, skill, talent, experience and intuition are equally important. Landing a muskie is an accomplishment. That doesn't mean that a beginner might not snag one through pure dumb luck, but the odds are against it. Your muskie accounts are the large local or regional customers. Everyone in your market may know of them. People outside of your market probably will not. Because they are larger more savvy accounts, it takes a skilled salesperson to land them. Landing them is a sport. To the aggressive muskie salesperson, the thrill and the challenge mean as much as the commission.

➤ Pan fish: These are the decent accounts that lie all over your territory. This is where the expression, "There's more fish in the sea" comes from. As long as you're out there working, you'll pick up a few and you'll lose a few. The goal is to work hard enough to pick up more than you lose. Unlike whales, no single account will make or break your numbers. Inexperienced salespeople like these accounts because they are typically easier to land and to handle once hooked. If you want to keep eating, however, you will need to continue trolling on a regular basis. There are two potential downsides.

o You may run out of prospects. Only a select number of industries offer an unlimited supply of pan fish prospects.

o   Time is the limiting factor. Remember, we're talking about raising your hourly wage. If your objective is to make more by signing more accounts, you'll be earning the same hourly wage while putting in a lot of overtime.

➤   Minnows: These are the tiny little accounts that most salespeople pay little attention to. It's no wonder they get so little attention: They hardly provide a snack, let alone a meal. Minnows are little more than bait, and you typically don't fish for them; you scoop them up in large quantities with a net. There's nothing wrong with scooping up a few little accounts while on the way to visit with your more strategic prospects and accounts. What is important, however, is that you work them in along the way and never let them take any time away from your planned activities. When selling to minnows, it's real simple and it's right now.

Using the following chart, picture where each prospect you're calling on might be categorized.

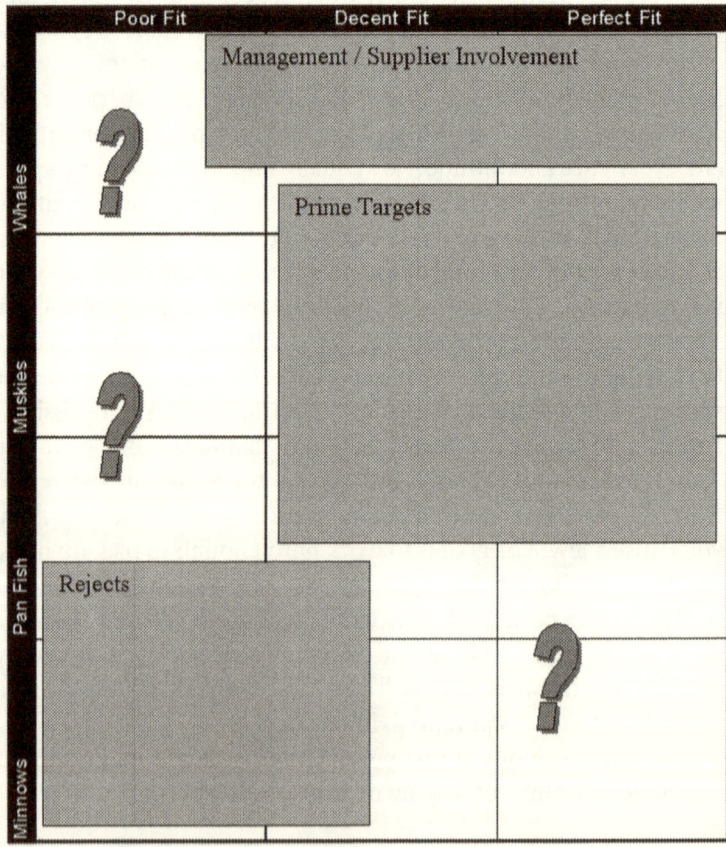

Notice that any prospect that is a poor fit with your organization and is comparatively small (minnows, small pan fish) will not help you reach your goals and should be eliminated from your prospect list.

In the opposite corner, a whale account that is a perfect fit with your organization must have manager and/or supplier involvement since these accounts will require someone to coordinate a great deal of infrastructure.

Between the perfect fit whales and the poor fit minnows are your prime targets. These are the accounts that have at least a decent fit with your organization and are large enough to be worth the time and energy. This is where you are most likely to find those accounts that will raise your hourly wage.

Whales and muskies that are a poor fit with your organization should be examined closely. A tremendously large account will almost certainly require a customized program. Just be certain that the customization is not so dramatic that it completely changes your company's focus. If it does, the existing business that got you to where you are today may be jeopardized.

I have also placed a question mark in the opposite corner for those accounts that are a perfect fit but are awfully small. These are great prospects to work into holes in your schedule, when you're in the area. They are the bonus accounts.

If you're compensated or evaluated based upon gross profit, these perfect fit minnows have a positive effect. A healthy company generally enjoys variety. Whales help drive market share, clout, horsepower and economies of scale, albeit at low gross profit margins. Pan Fish and Muskies are typically the core business, and minnows generally provide higher gross profit but have little impact on volume or horsepower. Truly effective companies generally enjoy a blend of all of these.

Hunters and Farmers

Sales activity can generally be separated into two categories, hunting and farming. Hunting, as the name implies, involves going out into the world, finding your prey, hunting it, catching it and dragging home the meat. Farming, on the other hand, is a much less aggressive method. Farmers plant seeds, nurture the soil and the plants, keep the fields moist and free from weeds and harvest the crop when it's ready. Since harvest time comes only a few times per year depending on the crops planted, farmers typically need to store some of their harvest to eat until the next harvest. Either method, hunting or farming, allow you to eat and to survive. They require very different skills and mindsets.

In selling, we use the term hunting as a metaphor for going out and landing new business. There is a thrill in the hunt. Hunting requires cunning, agility, speed, fitness, and energy. Hunters are typically thrill seekers who are bored to death looking out over a field waiting for something to grow. I was watching a nature special on PBS about crocodiles. The crocodile, it turns out, is among the most efficient predators on the planet. When a crocodile hunts, only a very small part of the crocodile can be seen above the water. It will creep up on a herd of large animals drinking from a river. The crocodile very slowly surveys the herd to determine which animal looks largest and easiest to catch. The crocodile does not thrash around showing off how tough it is, that would only alert its prey. Rather, it moves slowly and quietly toward it's chosen prey until it's absolutely certain it can grab it. When it does, it does not let go. I was surprised to learn that a crocodile can survive up to a year on a single animal if it's large enough.

I was struck by the similarity between the crocodile and the salesperson hunting for large accounts. Like a croc, a sales champion does not thrash around showing off. They're very quiet, very subtle. They survey all available prey until they determine which one best meets their objectives. They calmly but deliberately move in closer and closer until they know they can get it. When they grab it, they do not let go. Eating for the hunter is typically a matter of feast or famine. If they're good, there is a lot of feasting. If they are bad, they'll starve.

Ineffective salespeople tend to be conspicuous as they brag and boast. They thrash around from account to account hoping to catch one. The one they catch is usually the smallest or weakest and therefore they need to keep scrambling for more.

Farmers, on the other hand, do not wake up every morning yearning for the hunt. Farmers are more organized. They think ahead, take care of what they have and prepare for the lean months long after the harvest. A good farmer will ration the food in case next year's crop falls short. Farmers work hard and they're consistent. They'll study and test methods in their search for any improvement that might increase the yield even a fraction of a percent. If they're good, they'll always have something to eat, but it will never be an opulent feast. If they are bad, they too will starve.

There's a theory in selling that encourages companies to keep their hunters out landing new accounts then turning them over to the farmers to maintain. I have not seen this work very well. What tends to happen is the top accounts gradually slip. Since the salesperson that is assigned to maintain an account did not have to suffer the pain and frustration involved in landing the account, he or she goes into the process with less ownership. In addition, selling is about trust. Your new customer agreed to buy in large part because of you, the salesperson, and their trust in your ability to meet their needs. Turning the process over to someone new will only work if you assure your customer that you will continue to be actively involved in the account despite much of the routine daily activity being coordinated by your colleague.

Physics and the Prospecting Process

Here are three physical properties that are laws of nature. Like gravity, you don't get to decide whether or not you like them. They exist whether you like them or not. Understand them so that you can deal with them as they occur. Resistance is futile.

Inertia:

Inertia is sometimes referred to as momentum. The law of inertia tells us that an object in motion tends to stay in motion. An object at rest tends to stay at rest. Motivation is the process of moving someone from where they are to where you want them to be. If your prospect has been doing what they do the same way for a long time, a lot more energy will be required to move him or her. The same law applies to the way you've approached the sales profession. If you have been doing it the same way for a long time, rapid change will require a great deal of energy. When reviewing your prospects, don't expect an account who has a 20-year relationship with their current supplier to move as quickly as an account that has not been with any supplier more than a couple of years. When I say you need to make progress on every call, progress does not necessarily mean a presentation or commitment. Progress is any conversation or piece of information that gives you a clearer picture of what it's going to take to sign the account. Progress is also any indication that you are developing a closer relationship with your prospect and they are feeling more comfortable telling you about their world.

Also, when considering inertia, be aware that the size of the account will play a key role. The larger the account is, the more energy and time it will take to get them to change. In chapter 4 we discussed the need to migrate from smaller accounts to larger ones, so understanding this principle is crucial to your ultimate success.

How many sales calls does it take to get an account from cold call to active customer? You should have some number in mind. While it will vary from account to account, from one region to the next, and between industries, pick a starting point just to have something from which to build. Also, assume that we're talking about your average account. Stubborn accounts will take longer. For the sake of argument, let's say that it takes at least a couple of calls to determine who might have influence in the decision. Let's then assume that it takes at least two or three additional calls to learn what your prospect wants. It may take a dozen or more calls to exhume wants and needs. Do not short-cut this step. You'll never sign the account if you leapfrog this step hoping to get back to it. Next, we'll assume that it takes another two or three calls to get your customer to tell you how well your competitor is able to meet those desires. You then may need another call or two to identify specific problems and get your prospect to tell you that these are problems that they actually want to fix. Finally, you will need another sales call or two to propose solutions and a follow-up sales call to iron out concerns. The last call in this scenario will be your foot in the door. In all, I've just described a process that includes approximately 10 to 20 sales calls. If you're well organized and can generate enough interest from your prospect, you may be able to complete that process in 15 to 25 weeks depending upon availability, geography, and so forth. If your prospect is even mildly dissatisfied with their current supplier when you first stop in, the process will move more quickly. If you go from step one to the final step immediately, you should be very suspicious! If it looks too good to be true, it probably is.

Let's fine-tune that number. The principle of inertia tells us that a customer who is twice as stubborn may take twice as long. If that's the case, you may be looking at 30 weeks or more. Inertia also tells us that an account that's twice as large may take twice as long. If it's twice as large and twice as stubborn, you may be looking at 40 weeks or more! In some cases, it may take years. To exacerbate the problem, in these turbulent times, the company you're calling on may have a change of the guard in the process knocking you back to the beginning!

If you think I'm exaggerating, think again. Ask any of your highest performing peers how long it took from the first time they met their largest customer to the day they actually did business with them. In some cases, the time frame may be as long as 3 to 4 years! This is why you must track the progress you make on each call. Each wasted call extends the time it will take before you can enjoy the commission from the account. As you extend the process, your 5-year income goals become 7-or 10-year goals, and you lose more business to attrition in the process. Whether or not it's done consciously, this is one of the strongest reasons why so many competent salespeople shy away from large account solicitation.

With smaller accounts that can be signed in 3 to 4 months, most halfway intelligent people can remember enough of the basic facts long enough to keep the process moving forward. If the process takes a year or longer, you better have several in the hopper at any given time. Just try to keep the process moving forward with 6 or 8 of these large accounts and see if a year later you can actually remember what you've learned and what you still need to know. This is why the record cards described earlier are so vitally important for this effort. For mediocre salespeople the process becomes significantly less strategic as they just keep stopping by waiting for the decision maker of the corporate direction to change. This is a highly time consuming, hit-or-miss, low efficiency method that depends more on luck than strategy.

Inertia is a key principle in selling by the numbers. Assuming I've convinced you to focus on larger accounts by now, I'm hopeful that I have also convinced you of the concurrent need to start documenting your progress on each call. Start with a number, any number, as an estimate of how many calls should be required in order to take the average account from cold call to foot-in-the-door. Use the chart below to better understand this principle. Since there are so many factors influencing these milestones, this chart is for illustration only. I am not suggesting that your solicitation process will precisely fit these time lines.

What is important is that you develop an awareness of how long each of these steps should take for your unique circumstances. As stated earlier, if you don't know where you're going, you probably won't get there. As soon as you promote an account from suspect to prospect, lay out a series of target dates by which you plan to achieve each of these milestones. While never carved in stone, this activity will keep you on track helping you to make certain that you are making the best use of each visit. Keep inertia in mind as you lay out the time line. If the account is larger than your average account, expect it to take longer. If the account has been loyal to their existing supplier for a long time, expect them to be resistant to change and expect the process to take longer still.

Just don't make the mistake of leaving it open-ended and not tracking progress. I've worked with far too many good salespeople who got lost in the process and never quite realized just how long they'd been working on a given account. Each day that passes pushes you farther from your goal.

Prospecting time-line estimation

Milestone	Average Account	Stubborn Account	Stubborn, whale-type account
	Calls Projected		
Determine who has influence on the decision	2	3	8
Determine what they, as a group, want.	3	5	8
Confirm how well their wants are being satisfied	2	3	8
Expose problems that you can fix	1	2	4
Confirm that your prospects actually wants to fix the problems.	1	2	3
Propose solutions	1	2	3
Address and iron out concerns	1	2	4
Get foot in the door	1	1	2
Total	12	20	40

Velocity:

Velocity is just another word for speed. If you want to go far, you either have to take more time or go faster. Everyone has a comfort zone when it comes to speed. If you're the type of person who likes to go fast, it probably drives you nuts to be in the passenger seat when the driver likes going real slow. Conversely, if you prefer driving slowly, you're probably very uncomfortable when the driver of your vehicle drives real fast. Here, the math is fairly simple. If you move too quickly with solicitation of a slow moving prospect, you'll frighten them. They'll become uncomfortable and unavailable. Conversely, if you're moving real slowly with a prospect that's a "mover and shaker," they'll become frustrated. Like driving, it's when you go too fast or too slow that people tend to get out of the vehicle or are reluctant to ride with you again.

Notice that the principle of velocity or speed has two components, distance and time. When developing your projected time line, think about your proposal and how different it is from what they're doing now. Many salespeople tend to propose innovative solutions that are significantly different and supposedly better than their competitor's current offering. This is a double-edged sword. If your proposal is not much different from your competitor's, it's tough to build a case for change and there will be little urgency. On the other hand, if your proposal is dramatically different, you are asking your prospect to take a more formidable risk, so they'll need more time to consider all the ramifications.

Be aware of how much change you're asking your prospect to consider. If you're asking them to move far outside of their comfort zone, be prepared for the process to take longer. How much longer will depend on your prospect's comfort level with change. There are clues. Here is where strategic small talk can be of great value. What are their hobbies? Where have they lived? Where do they live now? Any tidbit of information concerning their comfort level with regard to change and risk is worth knowing.

It's also important that you match the speed at which your prospect likes to speak. People have a tendency to speak at the same pace that they prefer to listen. That's where the term fast-talker comes from. If you speak faster than your prospect prefers to listen, they may not absorb everything that you're saying. When that happens, your prospect will become uncomfortable as they become concerned that you slipped something into the conversation without them being aware.

Likewise, if you speak slowly, your prospect may interpret that as condescension. There's an old story about two salesmen taking a customer out to lunch. One salesman begins to tell a joke about some dummy from the state university. The second salesman stopped him and whispered, "Shhh, that's the college our customer graduated from!" The first salesman said, "Oh, that's okay, I'll tell the joke real slow." When you speak slowly to a prospect that moves more quickly you run two risks. They'll either think that you are slow or that you think they are slow. Either one will work against you. Match your customer's pace as best you can.

Acceleration:

Consider taking an airplane across the country. When you're on the runway prior to take off, you're nice and still. Then the pilot hits the thrust. He needs to get the airplane from zero to several hundred miles per hour, and he only has a short time in which to do it. This part of the trip is, for most people, either the most uncomfortable or the most exciting. If anything is going to go wrong with the journey, this is where it's most likely to happen! The only part of the trip that has a similar feeling is the landing. When the jet reaches a comfortable cruising altitude, you are actually traveling at a velocity near 500 miles per hour. Barring turbulence, even this speed feels nice and comfortable.

If a prospect had been reluctant at first but is now moving forward in the process, don't slow down. The toughest part is to get them moving. Once you do, be sure to keep them moving. If you start to slow down the process unexpectedly, most prospects will become uncomfortable. How quickly you accelerate should be geared to your prospect. They will give you pretty clear clues regarding their comfort level with regard to how rapidly they embrace change. If you hear statements like "Slow down," or "Gee, I don't know about that," you may consider slowing down a bit. Conversely, if your prospect asks you to "Get to the point," or begins a series of rapid-fire questions like, "How would that work?" "Who else uses it?" "How long has it been around?" you may be dealing with someone who has a need for speed.

"Cap'n, I cannot change the laws of physics"
—Mr. Scott (Star Trek)

To summarize prospecting physics, be sure to have at least a tentative timeline. It's critical that you track the results of each call and review them regularly to see that you stay on track. You don't determine the actual timeline, physics does; don't resist it. Don't try to rush it, and don't slow it down when you're on a roll. Stay flexible to the process. Be observant and watch for clues. Selling is about meeting wants and needs. More than anything, your prospect needs to feel comfortable throughout the process. Matching your solicitation to their buying pattern is the first and most important step in that process.

It's the Time of the Season

If you're in a seasonal business, there is an additional time management component that needs to be addressed and understood. It is illustrated in the following chart. During the slow months (in the example, I'm using February through May) business is slow for you because it's slow for your customer. Your company has more staff than it has business, so there isn't much that falls between the cracks. There is a large margin for error and any problems that pop up are recognized and corrected quickly. Your customers are fairly content since they don't need much, and you are poised to handle their needs promptly. Since your existing customers aren't busy, they're not very demanding. This leaves a lot of time for you to prospect for new business.

Unfortunately, it's the worst time to do prospecting. All of your competitors are in the same situation, so they're out prospecting as well. Next time you're out prospecting in the slow season, ask your prospect how many salespeople they saw in the previous two weeks. The answer may astound you. Compounding matters, not much is going on, so nearly every prospect you meet is apathetic. You hear a lot of "I do business with your competitor; everything is just fine." As I mentioned earlier, this apathetic inertia is among the toughest obstacles to overcome. They're not lying. During the slow period, your prospects' solution needs are low, and your competitor's infrastructure is ready and waiting to help.

When business starts to pick up (mid-year in this example), the average salesperson gradually fades out of prospecting activity and refocuses on his or her existing customers. Since their customer's solution needs are increasing, demands on the salesperson's time are on the rise. Afraid of leaving existing accounts vulnerable, they all but abandon their prospects until the next slow season.

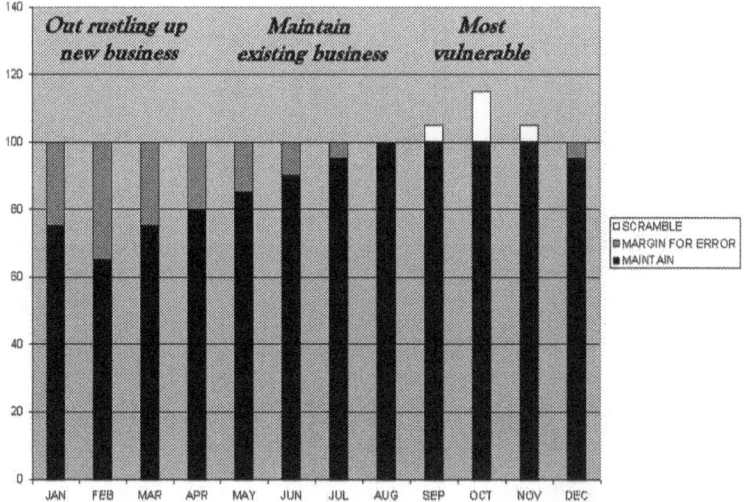

What's wrong with this picture? Selling is a process of identifying and addressing customer needs. In a seasonal business, most salespeople are in front of their prospect when solution needs are low and absent when solution needs are high. *Selling by the Numbers* is about effective time management. You need to be well organized so that, when the season hits, you have identified your most important prospects, developed a plan for focused consistent solicitation of those targeted prospects, and are committed to carrying out that plan. The slow season should be used for making as many cold calls as possible in an effort to distill a small, workable number of strategic targets.

8

Communication

"Seek first to understand, then to be understood."
—*Chinese Proverb*

Motivation Is What We Do, Communication Is How We Do It.

When you're in outside sales, being an effective communicator isn't everything; it's the only thing. I'm reminded of a "Take your daughter to work day" nearly 15 years ago. My young daughter and I spent the day making sales calls. Of course, on this day, I was not going to line up my toughest customers. Our first sales call went well. I discussed a new product with one of my better customers. We left, drove to the next city and called on another customer. When we finished that call, we went to one of my favorite customers and took him to lunch. When we finished eating, my daughter and I brought my customer back to his office and started heading toward the next sales call. My daughter looks over at me and asks, "So daddy, when are we going to your work?" Surprised at the question, I asked, "What do you think we've been doing all day?" She replied, "We've just been driving around talking to people." I asked, "Well, what is it you think I do all day for work?" And she replied, "That's what I was hoping to find out!"

Until that moment, I had not realized how peculiar a career in sales is. While some of us have a technical component to our job, at the end of the day, communicating with others is what we do. Too many salespeople think that communication is all about talking. Sure talking is part of the communication process. It's not the only part. In fact, it's not even the most important part. Communication has two components, giving and receiving. Communication can be verbal or non-verbal. Verbal communication can be vocal or written. Written is always better. When something is in print, it's more dependable. You can't say you never said it. If it's from an authoritative unbiased source, it will have an even greater impact. Communication is the art of transferring a message. The message needs to be credible if it is to be effective. As you consider how you are going to transmit the message, consider all methods available and decide which method is most likely to yield the results you seek.

When you show up on time, follow-up promptly, dress appropriately, and listen intently, you are communicating things about yourself. As you ponder forms of communication, remember that actions speak louder than words.

Before you start to think about how you're going to transfer the message, you must be crystal clear about what message you need to send. Your message is about change.

Recall that there are four ways to motivate change:

To encourage a behavior, "Do this and you will…"

➤ …get something you want.
➤ …lose something you don't want.

To discourage a behavior, "Stop doing this or else you will…"

➤ …get something you don't want.

➤ …lose something you want.

All of this is predicated on determining what your prospect wants. We do this through dialogue. Dialogue, by definition, is two-way communication back and forth. Far too many salespeople don't use dialogue, they use monologue. Monologue, of course is one way. "We have this many locations," "We carry these brands," "It has the following guarantee," and "It costs this much" are all examples of monologue. Dialogue is more engaging. Dialogue involves asking questions. If you do nothing more than increase the number of questions you ask, you'll be more successful even if you don't listen to the answers. Real, effective dialogue involves *at least* as much listening as it does talking. When you're telling, you're not selling. Asking questions shows that you care. Once you get in the habit of asking questions, you can steer each selling interview. It's impossible for you to describe how you'll meet their wants and needs until you know emphatically what their wants and needs are. The only way to find that out is through questions.

Since real dialogue involves at least as much listening as talking, all questions are not created equal. You must ask open-ended questions. Closed-ended questions work for closing sales. That's why they both contain the word *close*. But from the first chapter and throughout this book one message should be clear. In recurring business, your objective is not to close sales; rather it's to open relationships. This is a universal truth that applies whether you're trying to get a new customer or a new friend. Open-ended questions open up relationships.

Let me give you an example from early in my selling career where I learned this principle the hard way. I was a rookie manufacturer's rep for a tire company. One of my distributors asked me to ride with their new salesperson and show him how it's done. With my trainee in tow, we walked into our first suspect. Here's how the conversation went with the first person I saw.

I said, "Hello, we represent ABC Company. Is the tire buyer available?"
He answered, "Yes."
I said, "Who would that be?"
He said, "Me."
I said, "I see that you currently buy brand X."
He said, "Yep."
I asked, "Have you ever carried a brand other than brand X?"
He said, "Nope."
I asked, "Had you ever considered changing brands?"
His reply, "Mmmmm, nope!"

My final question was, "Would you ever consider changing brands?"
He said, "Nope!"
After a pregnant pause, I said, "Well then, thank you for your time, we'll see you later." And we left.

Let's run the numbers on that sales call. In all, I spoke 55 words. My suspect muttered six. That's a 9:1 ratio. What I did was close myself in. I came into the man's business armed with six questions that I like to refer to as *panels*. Subconsciously, it was a transparent attempt to use those *panels* to create a ceiling, floor, and four walls to box the prospect in. Instead, as often happens, he helped me box myself in. Once I did, I had nowhere to go! It was pretty embarrassing. It probably wouldn't surprise you to hear that I never went back. The box I put myself in was too tight to escape with any dignity, even after all of these years. I was attempting to close a sale. It was years before I realized that the objective was not to close sales but to open relationships. You can't open relationships by erecting walls; you do it by knocking walls down.

Your objective in recurring sales is not to close your prospect in. Even if it works, your prospect will become claustrophobic. Prospects will find a way to escape, and they won't give you an opportunity to do it again. Your objective is to help them get out of the box that they are currently in by opening up new worlds of opportunity for them. Open-ended questions come naturally when you're trying to open up the world for your prospect. This may sound counter-intuitive, but the fact remains. The very best communicators say very little. The only reason you talk is to open your prospects up and get them to talk about what's important to them.

Read that selling interview again and ask yourself, "Who's on stage?" Picture yourself attending a seminar in a room filled with hundreds, maybe thousands of people. Is the speaker likely to learn much about any individual member of the audience? Is he or she likely to learn any of their dreams and desires, their hopes and fears? Is there any way the speaker can learn what any individual wants out of life? No, the one who is listening is the one who is learning. An effective salesperson puts his or her prospect on stage and becomes the audience.

Once you've opened up your prospect, you must have good listening skills or you'll miss your opportunity. What most salespeople don't realize, however, is that good listening is not a skill in and of itself. The ability to be a good listener is rooted in confidence. I've already explained that communication involves so much more than just words. Listening to the words is the easy part. Catching all the subtle hints and interpreting body language is much more difficult. To do that, you must be completely in the moment. You must have all of your senses in tune with the environment and be free from distraction. As a rookie salesperson, that's very hard to do. If you are overly self-conscious, you'll be thinking about your last training meeting, the call that didn't go well earlier, your quota, that tough customer you're scheduled to see later, the competitor who is trying to get into your biggest customer, and so much more.

When you lack confidence, you tend to be unsure about your ability to come up with the right answers to your prospect's questions. Instead of paying attention to the interview at hand, while your prospect is talking you start to anticipate his or her questions and consider how you might answer them. If you're lucky, the prospect actually asks the question you thought he or she would ask, and before they have a chance to move on to something else, you jump in with your answer. You're excited because you actually did anticipate the question and you had an answer for it! This will lead to several problems.

➤ You were so deep in your own thoughts that you weren't really paying attention, so you inevitably miss a great deal of the communication.

➤ Subconsciously, your prospects can tell that you're doing it. They get the feeling that you aren't really paying attention and that your mind is somewhere else.

➤ People will often begin with a gentle list of objections to keep the conversation "safe." In the early stages of the selling process, your prospect may feel uncertain about the purchase, but has not yet completely figured out why he or she is feeling uncomfortable. He or she knows instinctually that, if they offer this primary concern before they've had a chance to crystallize the thought, they'll be forced to defend it. So they throw out gentler objections. If you sit and listen, your prospect may rattle off several in a row. Sometimes, given enough space, they'll answer their own question. Try it, it happens. In addition, by the mere fact that they're throwing out a list, it becomes obvious that several of the objections were not really germane to the decision. They were, at best, stray thoughts.

➤ Addressing each objection the minute it pops out will lead to the sparring match described in chapter 2. This is the very worst place to be. Once you start sparring, if you make the sale, you win, they lose. If you don't make the sale, they win, you lose. You do not want your prospect to be in a position where they feel like they win only if they prevent you from selling them something.

A common theme in the above is a lack of confidence. Confidence comes from a deeply rooted sense of purpose. If you are completely committed to helping your customers get what they want out of life, having all the right answers becomes secondary. You learn that having the right questions is more important. When you are completely engaged in the moment, you hear what has not been said. You clarify by asking questions like, "I hear what you're saying but I'm not sure that I completely understand what it is you're looking for. Can you tell me more?" Not only does this let you off the hook for not having an answer, it shows your prospect that you are different, that you are thorough and professional, and that you care. It puts your prospect in the spotlight where they ought to be. You are the student, not the teacher. It also smacks of humility. Arrogant salespeople will never say that they don't fully understand. To them it's a sign of weakness. The champion understands the importance of revealing weakness. Real emotional strength is demonstrated when you are confident enough to reveal your weaknesses.

To do this effectively, you must learn to READ your prospect. Notice I did not say READ your suspect. You don't move into this phase of the process until you've promoted the account from suspect to prospect. Once you do, you must start a card on them like the account record card illustrated earlier in this book. READing your prospect involves gathering all the information you'll need to get your foot in the door.

Reading Your Prospect

Reconnaissance: (Before the Sales Call)
Reconnaissance is the process of learning as much as you can about your prospect's situation without having to ask them. The more we know before the first call, the more effective it will be. Not only does it send a message to your prospect that you are knowledgeable, professional, and prepared, it conveys a message that you respect your prospect's time. It also helps you to steer the conversation in the direction you want to go right off the bat, instead of flowing with the tide and hoping you like where you wind up. Reconnaissance involves asking yourself four basic questions prior to the sales call.
> What do I already know?
> What do I think I know but need confirmation?
> What do I still need to know?
> Where might I get that information without having to bother my prospect?

In today's information age, if you don't have Internet access, get it and learn how to use it. At the very least, find a library where you can go to access it. You will be amazed at how much information you can learn prior to a meeting. With a click of a mouse, you can get information on your customer's business, their industry, their marketplace, your competitors, the business climate, and so much more. In addition to the Internet, your peers, other customers, trade press, and industry associations are terrific sources of information that will help you with the process. Don't second-guess what information is or is not important. It won't be until you're deep in conversation with your prospect that you'll uncover a need for the information.

In general, the information you seek will fall into two categories.

➢ What can this customer do for you and your organization?
➢ What can you do for this customer?

Certainly, reconnaissance is the best way to learn answers to the first question, "What can this customer do for you and your organization?" Remember that most salespeople are considered predators and their prospects feel like prey. When a salesperson walks through the door, buyers instinctually feel protective and wonder, "What is he or she going to try to get out of me?" That's why your prospects become so irritated when you ask qualifying questions like, "How many units do you buy each year?" "How many locations do you have?" "How many pieces of equipment do you operate?" "What are your future expansion plans?" or "How many employees do you have?" The answer to these questions is of little or no value to your prospect, only to you. They are self-serving. When you ask them, you are asking your prospect to invest his or her time enhancing your future. Successful salespeople do things in reverse. They invest their time to enhance their prospect's future. That's why it's so important to learn what you can without having to ask your prospect. If each of your sales interviews is focused on what's important to your prospect, the calls will flow much better. You will show your customer that you are a professional when you tell them what you've already learned about their organization by doing your own research, and it shows that you care.

Furthermore—and here's where it gets interesting—initial reconnaissance provides clues to what your prospect might want. Once you visualize several things that they might want, you can develop questions to determine if your prospect actually wants any of those things. That's why you need to develop an agenda prior to each call. You can plan on exactly what you hope to learn. You'll also anticipate the answers so that you can be prepared. It's like playing the game, Battleship. You think about where you might find your opponent's ship and call off coordinates hoping for a hit. Once you have a single hit, you know to fish around in the same general vicinity until you nail the vessel. When anticipating a response, I like having a three-tiered approach. What is the best-case scenario of this visit, the least acceptable, and the most likely? The best case, of course, is a hit. Your prospect says, "Yes, that's exactly what I need.

Do you have that?" Before you ask the question, make sure you can answer it positively. The most likely scenario is a miss, but you learn a little more about where not to look. The least acceptable response is hitting a nerve. If your prospect gets insulted by your question and ends the meeting, you've got a problem. Before asking a question, be sure to consider the worst-case scenario. Please note that I said to be prepared. I did not say to be "canned" and rigid. Preparation is very important, but don't get carried away. There's a distinct difference between a canned presentation and a well-planned presentation. A canned presentation is a one-size-fits-all generally used in one-shot sales efforts like telemarketing. A well-planned presentation is custom fit to the prospect's needs and wants. Questions for a well-planned presentation come from preliminary investigation and consideration specific to that prospect. If it works, a canned presentation will capture the interest quickly, close the sale immediately and end the relationship upon completion. It requires a virtually unlimited base of prospects and is used only when you have one chance to make or break the sale. That's why it's called closing the sale! If you fail miserably, it's no big deal because there are plenty more fish in the sea.

Conversely, a planned presentation is not a variation of that process; it is the polar opposite! An effective planned presentation will open the relationship and allow you, the salesperson, to move in. You won't just move in further, you'll move in closer. This is why it's so difficult. Your prospect doesn't initially want you to get closer. At least not until you've earned their trust. The closer you get, the more vulnerable they will feel. If you are asking pointed questions and your prospect starts to get nervous and edgy, you're probably getting close. Think of your prospects going through their day dealing with their crises when you show up at the door. Their first response is to put up their shields. At first blush, you are a salesperson, and a potential predator. They have money or they wouldn't still be in business. You want their money or you wouldn't be there, would you? Before they put the defense shields down, they'll want to know who you are and what you want. You still won't make it past their defenses until they believe that there's some chance you can help them. Visiting over and over before you convince them that you might be of value is just an attempt to wear down the defense shields.

If you are successful wearing down their defense shields prior to establishing your value, one of several things happened.

> ➢ Their defense shields were not very strong, and you broke through them with sheer will and determination. If this is the case, you should be concerned, very concerned. It's an indication that if and when you get the business, it may not be all that hard for your competition to break through the same shields and take it from you.

➤ If it was unusually easy to break through their defenses, be alert to signs that there may be no money there for your prospect to protect. Even when a company does not pay their bills, they may still need the product you're selling. Letting you past their shields turns the tables. No one else will sell to them, but you don't know that. You're blinded by the fact that your incredible sales prowess broke through like a hot knife through butter. Wow, you're good. Then once they have you on their turf lulled into a false sense of security fed by your own ego, they turn the tables. Now it's you who is trying to protect your assets, your capital. They suckered you in and now they won't pay. Very simply, if it seemed too easy, there's probably a good reason.

➤ You got lucky. There was a tiny weak spot in the shield. Let's assume that your prospect's current supplier is a decent competitor. Even the very best are not perfect. Many salespeople hope that by visiting frequently enough and talking long enough, they will eventually stumble upon their competitor's weakness and break through. It happens. Unfortunately, since it's generally by luck, it's almost impossible to duplicate. So as a salesperson, you just take that success and go to the next prospect and try the same approach. Not only is it incredibly time consuming, but also prospects tend to tire of it rather quickly. It's like the nagging mosquito. You just know that if you let it continue to buzz around something will eventually distract you. The second you do, it zooms in and sucks out your blood. How do you keep that from happening? You swat the thing and kill it.

Reconnaissance doesn't end when you walk into your prospect's office. It has only just begun. Remember that your objective is to learn as much as you can about what is important to your prospect throughout the process. The more you can learn without having to ask, the more likely you are to keep the interview from turning into an interrogation.

Once in the door, look around and see what else you can learn about them. Are they well organized? Do they display evidence of hobbies? Do they have anything from your competition on the walls or on their desk? I've been in numerous sales calls where my competitor's invoice is just laying on their desk! Look closely at any pictures. You may see a photo of your prospect in a golf tournament with your competitor. That's an important clue about the relationship, don't you think? You might see photos of your prospect engaged in some sport or hobby that you or one of your existing customers also enjoys. What a great way to provide a connection that might lead to a testimonial.

Try to catch them in conversation with their boss. Examine their dialogue. Do they have autonomy? Do they need approval from their supervisor regarding even simple decisions? Do the people that interact with them look to them for solutions? Does he or she take quick decisive action or do they like to "think about it"? Ask about some of the other products they use that aren't related to yours. Why do they choose to use those products?

These are all important clues that you will later use when delivering solutions.

Examination: (During the Sales Call)

This is where it all happens. This is where you find the pain. Picture walking into your doctor's office saying, "Doc, I have the following condition, and this is how I want you to treat it." First of all, it doesn't usually happen that way since most patients only know that they hurt. They rarely know the precise cause and even more rarely are completely informed regarding current methodology for treatment. That's what they pay doctors for. Secondly, any real doctor who wants to continue practicing medicine won't perform any procedure until he or she confirms the cause and evaluates all possible treatment methods. There is an old analogy in business that goes something like this: Prescription without diagnosis is malpractice. If you went to a doctor and he or she started to prescribe a treatment for you before going through a complete examination, how likely would you be to follow that treatment? You would consider that doctor to be a quack.

The fact-finding process used in professional selling is very similar. Too often, I've seen ineffective salespeople walk into a prospect's office and ask, "Do you need anything?" Only to become depressed when the tenth prospect in a row says, "No, I think I'm in pretty good shape!" Even on a routine checkup, a doctor starts by asking a few standard questions. He or she generally records vitals such as pulse, blood pressure, weight, and so forth. Using a stethoscope, he or she will listen to your lungs and, with a small light, look into your eyes and/or your ears. If he or she notices something a little bit out of the ordinary, they'll generally ask you, "How long have you had this?" or "Does it hurt when I do this?" During a checkup, your doctor is trying to find any abnormality before it becomes severe enough for you to have a problem. He or she may find something vague and just decide to keep an eye on it. Between the initial discovery and your next office visit, you will be thinking about what was found. You may now notice minor discomfort in that area that you hadn't paid any attention to previously.

This is how the most powerful sales transactions take place. You, as a "sales doctor" should not be asking, "Do you need anything?" You should be performing a business health checkup. Like medicine, selling has fundamental vital signs. And there are four terrific questions that you can use to get the diagnosis started.

➤ Whom do you currently buy from?
➤ How long have you been buying from them?
➤ Whom did you buy from previously?
➤ Why did you switch?

Like pulse, blood pressure, and weight, these four questions are totally non-invasive, non-threatening and provide important clues. Once you determine who your competitor is, ask yourself these four important questions.

➤ What do they do well?
➤ What do they do poorly?
➤ What is your competitive edge?
➤ What types of accounts do they typically target?

If you know your competitor well, you should have some ideas regarding what the prospect may not be happy with. If you know any accounts that used to do business with your competitor, ask why they quit.

When you ask, "Whom do you currently buy from?" you may learn that they buy from many different suppliers depending upon price. Pretty important clue, don't you think? You may learn that they buy primarily from ABC company, the most advanced competitor you have, but they also buy from XYZ in order to keep ABC honest. That tells you that you might be able to squeeze a foot in the door by gaining the number two position. Gaining the number two position is a low-risk way to get the prospect on board. You've also learned that, since their primary vendor is the industry leader, you will need to be sharp.

When you ask, "How long have you been buying from them?" you gain even more valuable insight. If they've been with their current supplier for a very short time, you can anticipate that there may not be a strong loyalty built yet. On the other hand, they may still be in the honeymoon period where everything looks rosy and wonderful. If you learn that they've been with the same supplier since before your contact person started with the company, you can surmise that the decision maker is at least one step over his or her head.

If the answer is, "I've been with them for many years, and I don't have any reason to switch," they are saying, in effect, "If it isn't broke, why fix it?" More salespeople that I've worked with have difficulty deciding where to go from here than from any other objection. The answer lies in basic human nature. For most of us, the longer we have something, the more we take it for granted. If you don't believe me, watch PBS and notice how much of the world lives in persecution and abject poverty with no opportunity for improvement in their lifetime. Then ask if we, as Americans, take our freedom, opportunity, and quality of life for granted? Most of us do. The longer we have something, the more likely we are to take it for granted. If your competitor has enjoyed this account's loyalty for a long time, they will take the account for granted.

Raising the Bar

Your objective is to raise the bar that your competitor must jump over each day. You can do this while complimenting them. Try to determine at least five features that your prospect is likely to agree is most important to them.

Here's how you phrase it: "Mr. Prospect, we do business with many companies similar to yours, and I've developed an awareness of what many of them feel are the most critical issues specific to the type of product/service I represent." Then, with your prospect's permission, list the features and ask your prospect for confirmation of their importance. Ask if there are additional issues of equal or greater importance, then agree that they are very important issues. Confirm in no uncertain terms that they should be able to depend on their supplier to effectively address those critical issues.

Then comes the most important part. It is also the part that most salespeople do wrong. Pay close attention to this approach. It will change your life. Do NOT proceed to tell your prospect why you're better than your competitor at addressing those issues. This comes across as nothing more than salesman rhetoric and lip service. Not only do your words have little value, you'll only make them defensive and move farther away from the relationship you're trying to build. Once you uncover the most important issues, ask for a follow-up meeting so that you can describe how you and your company address those issues.

For the follow-up meeting, bring in testimonials, examples and any other hard evidence that supports how well you address these key issues. You must have some form of objective evidence supporting how you address the issues if you want them to have meaning. After (and it absolutely must be after) each solution you present, you should say something like, "I know my competitor is strong; they must have an equally effective way of handling this. Do you mind if I ask how they do it?" If they don't know, you've just gained some ground. You've planted the first seed of doubt. Don't be surprised if they defend your competitor's methods. When they do, compliment them. Before you leave, you must secure the most critical advance. You must ask for permission to stop in from time to time to learn as much as you can about their organization so that you can completely understand their wants and needs in case there is anything you might ever be able to do to help. Depending on your line of work, an ideal advance is permission to inspect their operation and gauge the performance of the different products that they are now using.

By the time you've addressed each issue and illustrated your solution, you will have raised their expectations of their current supplier. There's no telling how long it might take for your competitor's shortcomings to be exposed, but they will be exposed. Picture what's going on in your prospect's mind. They've confirmed for you and for themselves what is most important. They've seen you prove that you can effectively address each issue. They begin to visualize meetings with their current supplier whom they have believed to be addressing the issues all along. Since they're comfortable with their current supplier, it's unlikely that they've held regular meetings inspecting their work. Your prospect has trusted your competitor, and your competitor has taken them for granted.

Now all it takes is for your prospect to have a few spare minutes to see if they're actually getting what they pay for from your competitor. Rest assured, if you've done everything I've recommended thus far, your prospect will begin to view your competitor's performance much more critically. Inevitably, they will find at least one or two small matters that need to be addressed. Each time an issue is exposed, your prospect's loyalty to your competitor drops, and your chances improve. In many cases, they find so many inconsistencies with your competitor that they may boot them out altogether and immediately.

Most salespeople that I've worked with get depressed when they meet a great prospect that is staunchly loyal to their current supplier, and they shouldn't be. Don't be afraid to tell your prospect how much you appreciate and admire that loyalty. An effective approach sounds something like this: "Like ABC company, we also enjoy this level of loyalty from some of our best customers." (You just implied that your prospect, if signed, would be given top priority as a best customer and you showed that you'll appreciate them if and when they sign up.) Then find some small insignificant piece of the business where your competitor may be falling short. It will be your foot in the door. Your prospect may just be willing to give you that "nasty" little piece of the business that their primary supplier didn't really want. They may even believe that they're doing your competition a favor.

Then, when you shine, you're sending a clear message that, "If I do so well on this tough stuff (the bitter vegetables) just imagine how great we'll do with the core business (the sweet dessert). The fiercely competitive business environment that we function in today doesn't allow for large staffs of people to hold things together. Your customers, therefore, have come to expect a certain level of chaos and disarray. When your prospect says, "Your competitor is doing just fine," he or she is not saying, "They don't ever make mistakes." They're really just saying, "Of all my most pressing crises, this isn't one of them. Why would I take a chance on switching and risk upsetting that piece?" By getting your foot in the door to alleviate one of their ancillary, low-risk aggravations, you have a chance to shine. Once they start to see you as a valid option (and this takes time), they will start to notice every time your competitor makes a small error, fails to return a call promptly or make something happen, and so forth. In the prospect's mind, they're saying, "I bet you would have called me right back, wouldn't you?" Your answer: "You bet I would!"

If your prospect is apathetic toward you because of loyalty to the current supplier, being taken for granted is your hidden opportunity. Be very careful how you go about trying to expose it. Telling someone that they're being taken for granted is an insult both to that person and to the person accused of taking them for granted. Long-term business relationships are personal relationships. You must proceed very gingerly when trying to expose being taken for granted. I like to start with a positive, sincere compliment: "It's nice to meet a loyal customer; in these fiercely competitive and uncertain times, I meet fewer and fewer each day. Fortunately, we too enjoy that kind of loyalty from several of our best customers. Conscious of just how rare they are, we go the extra mile to be exceptionally responsive to their needs and requests. I'm sure my competitor is that way to you *aren't they?* As good as they are, there may be a time when your back is against the wall and you need a back-up supplier. If that ever happens, please don't hesitate to call me. I'll do what I can to help."

This type of dialogue only works if it is sincere. It works for several reasons. First, it illustrates the type of care and attention they should be receiving from your competitor in exchange for the loyalty. Rest assured, you have just raised the bar the competitor will have to jump over. Secondly, every time they leave a message for their current supplier and the call is not returned immediately, your prospect will notice. Your prospect may be saying to himself or herself, "I bet this new salesperson wouldn't take two days to call me back." Of course, if they do call you, return the call IMMEDIATELY! The worst thing that you can do is to cop an attitude. It can be difficult to distinguish between your prospect abusing you only when their favorite supplier lets them down versus them giving you a few opportunities to prove yourself worthy of the risk involved in changing suppliers. Any foot in the door is worthwhile. If possible, never make it an either-or proposition. If your prospect can throw any piece of business your way without jeopardizing his or her relationship with the incumbent supplier, it's worth taking.

Of course, this can also work against you. Be very careful that you do not take your loyal customers for granted. Respond to their concerns just as you would to that brand new customer you spent years to land. That's one of the benefits to *Selling by the Numbers*. Almost immediately, you'll identify which customers you cannot afford to lose. You will not take them for granted. Over time, you will eventually distill your active customer list down to a smaller, more intimate base. With a smaller customer base, you're less likely to take them for granted.

"Whom did you buy from previously?" is a great question in context with the first two. If their current and previous suppliers are heavily service oriented, you can figure that service will be the primary decision factor. If both suppliers were price leaders, you know what you may have to do to get their attention.

Hands down, my favorite question is, "Why did you switch?" There is no better indication of what your prospect is looking for in a supplier. Did they switch because of service issues? Did they switch because a lower price came along? Did they switch because of a defect, warranty, or product quality issue? These are important clues. If they switched because the person you're talking to replaced a buyer that retired, you know that you're talking to a decision maker. Conversely, if your contact person says "I don't know, someone above me made that decision," that's good to know.

Communication is a journey from the general to the specific. If one of your first questions is "What do I need to do to earn your business today?" you're jumping the gun. These four "vital sign" questions simply start you on your way. Where you go from there will depend entirely upon the answers to those questions.

The "examination" process involves asking a lot of questions, considering the answers, uncovering symptoms, looking for patterns, and narrowing down the causes. As your questioning uncovers problems, your diagnosis will become more specific. Once you see an effective treatment, you need to question how likely your prospect will be to follow the recommendations and whether or not your prospect agrees that it might solve his or her problems.

Throughout the examination, be sure to take notes. The only notes I write when directly in front of the prospect are small details, numbers, cities, and so forth (The kind of details you need to know, but may not be able to recall after you walk out). While you don't want to interrupt the flow of the conversation by getting overly wrapped up in transcription, you surely don't want to ask the same question that your prospect already answered!

What if you've performed a thorough diagnosis and can't find any pain? Remember the old adage, "no pain no gain." If your prospect does not feel that anything is wrong, he or she is not likely to listen to your suggested treatment. This is one of the most common and most difficult obstacles. It is referred to as inertia.

Is it possible that there really is no pain and therefore no opportunity? That answer is NO! After being in sales for over 25 years, I have not met anyone who doesn't have something, however minor, that couldn't be better. There is always some pain. While finding the pain may be a challenge, it's often a greater challenge driving that pain until your prospect agrees that they need to do something to correct it. More likely, if you can't uncover the pain, your diagnostic skills need improvement. More specifically, your prospect probably has not yet come to trust you enough to share important information.

Make no mistake about it, even if you find the pain, you will not be successful selling a solution until the prospect has agreed that he or she wants to fix it. All too often we find a problem and we jump right in with a solution and then wonder why the prospect didn't leap up, shake our hand and yell, "YES, FINALLY!" Here's a critical point that you must understand. It's not enough to find your prospect's problem. You must get confirmation that your prospect wants to fix the problem before you offer a solution. Even if your prospect recognizes the problem, he or she may be reluctant to go through all that they'll have to do to remedy it. Until your prospect has admitted that they are determined to solve the problem, potential solutions will fall on deaf ears.

The four opening diagnostic questions provide clues, that's all. You will need to work off of these clues to find problems and opportunities and then, most importantly, get confirmation that the problem is something that your prospect actually wants to fix. I can't stress this point strongly enough. I've seen more really good salespeople hit a wall at this point than anywhere else in the selling process. The worst part is that they typically can't figure out why it happened. Up until this point, the process was going so well. The prospects told you they had a problem, you had a solution and they still said no!

Once you learn who the competitor is, if you know the competitor well, here are the types of questions that I've had good luck with. Used properly, they help steer the sales interview in your direction.

- ➤ I'm familiar with that company, I hear they do this well. Do you find that to be the case?
- ➤ How important is that to you?
- ➤ How are they in terms of this other thing?
- ➤ How important is that to you?

These questions are good for several reasons. They show that you are keenly aware of your competition. That adds to your credibility. Furthermore, if you choose an aspect that your competitor is not very good at, you invite your prospect to blast them so you don't have to. Remember from earlier in the book, you never want to blast your competitor. Perhaps most importantly, it begins to smoke out what is and is not important to your prospect. Without that knowledge, you simply won't make the sale.

Analysis: (After Each Sales Call)

The most important notes are the ones you make immediately following a sales call when you're out of the line of fire. If you are a procrastinator, this will be a tremendous obstacle to your success. If you wait until the end of the week to regurgitate the information, important facts learned in that presentation will surely be lost.

If you were strong and you resisted the temptation to start offering solutions so far, this stage is where you'll put the real power in the presentation. Review what you've learned from the previous calls. Take a few moments and ask yourself if you have enough information to make a presentation that is powerful enough to get your prospect to switch. Play devil's advocate. What obstacles is your prospect likely to bring up while you present? How will you overcome those obstacles? If you come up with obstacles that you can't overcome, don't go forward with the presentation hoping they won't get brought up. If they do, you're sunk. If this is an important prospect, ask someone to role-play. Ask them to be tough and come up with every possible obstacle they can think of. Be aware that, for your prospect, the next step in the psychological process is likely to be fear of change. Don't underestimate the gravity of the risk. The larger your prospect is, the more resistant they will be to change. More people are likely to be impacted by change. With a small prospect, you may be talking to the owner. If the company is small enough for the owner to have hands-on involvement in the entire operation, he or she can try something, see how it works, and change back if there are problems.

In a large company, there are many people involved in the decision. Large companies depend on effective integrated systems, so decisions rarely impact a single department. A failed program may have far-reaching implications. Here, your prospect will be looking to you to help them feel confident about your ability and commitment to make it through the inevitable implementation challenges. Throughout the preparation, continue to consider to whom you will be presenting. You must not only convince your immediate contact of your proposal, you must thoroughly train them to convince the influencers that you may never meet. Try to determine who all the influencers are and their proximity to the purchase. It's helpful to know how each of them will be affected by a change, whether they will help or hurt you, and as much as you can learn about your competitor's relationship with each of them. If you can, determine what, if anything, each of the influencers knows about you, your company, and your products. This is one of the toughest and most overlooked aspects of large account solicitation. These hidden influencers often make or break the decision.

Most importantly, after each call ask yourself if you have captured the heart. Does the prospect indicate that, on some level, he or she **wants** to do business with you? Whether or not you have addressed all of their concerns is secondary. Until you have captured the prospect's heart, presentations are fruitless. You need your prospect to be so excited about your proposal that they can and will sell it to the hidden influencers within their organization. If you have captured the heart, you need to ask yourself if you have provided the logic that the prospect will need to rationalize the decision. This will help them overcome the objections that they will face when presenting your solution to others. Some of that can be addressed with a formal presentation. If you're selling to a large company, you need to be sure that your contact person understands your material well enough to sell it to others in his or her organization who may be involved in the decision. Deep-seated concerns must be smoked out and addressed prior to a formal presentation. Analyze what you've learned thus far and ask yourself the following questions:

➢ What do I already know?
➢ What do I think I know but need confirmation?
➢ What do I still need to know?
➢ Where might I get that information without having to bother my prospect?

Delivery:

Whether or not this is a final presentation is not important. If you've done everything right so far, each follow-up meeting should include some reinforcement of concerns addressed in earlier meetings. When you deliver evidence supporting the concerns, keep it real, keep it honest, keep it pertinent and to the point.

You must be providing solutions to issues that your prospect wants to fix, and they must, at least, get your prospect intrigued. This is where it all comes together. If you took effective and complete notes after each call, planned calls in advance, and examined your position as you went along, you should be able to deliver a powerful presentation.

From what you've learned, describe for your prospect the issues that he or she faces. Ask for agreement along the way, that you have effectively described the issues relative to the current state of their business. Be sure to include both positive and negative issues. In scientific terms, it's said that every action has an equal and opposite reaction. Your prospect may accept your solution to the stated issue at-hand and still be reluctant to change for fear of how it might adversely impact other aspects of his or her business. Once they've agreed, **confirm that these are issues that they truly want to fix.** It's funny, most salespeople typically ignore the previous sentence as unimportant chatter when it is among the most important aspects of the selling process. If you gain nothing else from this book than the discipline to be absolutely certain that the stated issue is one that your prospect **wants** to fix, this book and the time you spent reading it will pay for itself. Then and only then should you describe how you plan to address those issues.

Think outside of the box. Innovative solutions will get your prospect's attention. In the words of Abraham Maslow, "Every really new idea looks crazy at first."

This is the moment of truth, and I'm not speaking metaphorically. This is not the time to promise more than you can deliver. Since most industries have become fiercely competitive, buyers are becoming very sophisticated and increasingly skeptical. They have built in lie detectors, so keep it real, keep it honest, keep it pertinent and to the point.

By this point, you've determined the problems, confirmed your prospect's sincere desire to fix the problems, and you've developed a powerful and effective solution. As you prepare to deliver your solution, try to step outside yourself and imagine being in the buyer's shoes. See if you can come up with a dozen or so reasons why your solution will not work. This can be difficult for salespeople since they tend to be optimistic by nature. All too often, I've been with salespeople who were so excited about their innovative solution that they did not even consider the possibility of the prospect saying, "No"! Every time it happened, the salesperson was speechless having no idea where to go next. It can be a very uncomfortable situation. The more prepared you are, the more confident you'll be. Your confidence in the effectiveness of the proposed solution will directly impact your prospect's confidence. Preparedness breeds confidence, plain and simple.

Persistence Pays!

With the complexity often associated with changing suppliers, your prospect knows that there will be some glitches along the way. Don't pretend that there won't be. It will diminish your prospect's trust if they don't feel that you recognize the potential risks as clearly as they do. Your job in the sales process is to assure your prospect that you fully understand their business, have anticipated those glitches, and are prepared to handle them quickly and effectively. He or she also needs to feel confident that you have the courage and tenacity to be there to work through any problems. Some buyers will intentionally blow you off several times just to see if you keep coming back. When you do, you're showing your prospect that you're a person of substance who will stick with it through the tough times. This trait, alone, will separate you from the sea of salespeople fighting for their business.

Reading a Whale

There's a significant difference between whales and smaller accounts. If you're talking to headquarters, the person you're talking to is typically far removed from the place where the pain is. The branch location feels the pain from the decisions made at HQ but is powerless to make changes. The location may think HQ doesn't care, but they can't see the bigger picture. HQ may care but can't respond to dozens or even hundreds of individual requests. They must maintain consistency and economies of scale in order to be effective and competitive. Selling to a whale is more complex. You'll need to work every angle from the top to the bottom. If you're talking to HQ, ask them for permission to visit the locations to better understand how they operate. You must assure them that you do not plan to sell the branch locations anything. You just want to learn more about their operation. If you're talking to the branch location, ask permission before going over their head. Watch for hidden opportunity and watch for land mines. Uncover them now. If you don't, they'll get you later. Figure out who can help you and who will resist you.

Reconnaissance

Reconnaissance with whales is more time consuming. It's also the most important piece of the puzzle. You must learn what they themselves may not even know. That's where you'll find your foot in the door. This is getting easier as business gets more competitive. As layers of middle management get eliminated, restructured, and downsized, the connections that were in place to keep HQ informed disconnect. You need to get to as many of the outlying locations as possible. You never know when you'll run into someone who will tell you what you need to know. There's more information available on whales. Because they're so big, you can learn a lot about them from the Internet and trade press. If they're large enough, you can even get information from the mass media. If you are a distributor of products, you might be able to gain important information from the manufacturers that supply to you.

Examination

Examination is a multi-pronged approach with whales. The same principles apply, but the examination is widespread. You must speak with as many people as you can get in front of within the organization. The higher you can get, the better. The lower ranks are also important. You might find pain in the most unlikely places.

Analysis

Analysis takes on new dynamics with whales since you learn pieces of the puzzle from the most unexpected places. You will need to compare what you learn from each source and see if you can visualize the whole picture. As an outsider, this type of analysis gives you an opportunity to see problems and solutions that are too difficult to see from the inside. There's a critical additional step. With big companies come big politics. You must analyze the situation well enough to anticipate whom you might threaten with any potential solution that you propose. If you don't, that person will become a sniper in the weeds. Your proposal might hit a brick wall, and you won't even know why.

For example, if you propose a solution that will streamline billing efficiencies, there might be people in the accounting department who will lose their jobs. You must find out if any one of those people will have influence in the decision. If they do, you must be prepared to navigate that land mine.

Delivery

Delivery is more complex when presenting to a whale. There are a lot of what-ifs. As you begin to expose opportunities, you need to start asking contacts throughout the organization how each suggestion will impact them personally. Throughout this section, I spoke of getting your foot in the door. Every large organization will have locations that just aren't up to par. If you have a potential solution, implementing it in these inefficient locations will be a low-risk proposition for your prospect. Your presentation will sound something like, "Here's a example of the worst-case scenario within your organization. What I propose surely can't make it any worse."

I can give you dozens of examples of tough prospects stuck in inertia that had no problem giving me a shot in their toughest outlying locations. They don't feel bad about taking those locations away from your competitor because your competitor isn't getting the job done out there anyway. Moreover, your competitor won't fight real hard to keep those outlying locations for two reasons. First, more often than not, they're happy to get rid of them. These trouble spots represent most of the frustration they have with the account. Second, fighting to keep those locations will inevitably lead to a difficult conversation about how they plan to fix the problem. What your competitor may not consider is how badly you can embarrass them once you get your foot in the door in these tough spots.

This scenario highlights how companies tend to take their loyal customers for granted. When you do business with a large whale account, it's not unusual to believe that 95 percent effectiveness is something to be proud of. That's really nothing more than a rationalization for failure to handle the problems representing the 5 percent. Anyone can handle the easy stuff. What differentiates champions from the mediocre majority is their ability to come through at crunch time when the going gets tough. As the old expression reads, "Did you ever notice that good enough rarely is?"

You must be very careful when deciding who to present solutions to and how to present them. If a mid-level influencer (called a sponsor) has given you an important piece of the puzzle, ask him or her how to best share that with people higher up in the organization who have the ultimate purchase authority and ask permission to quote them directly. You may find that your sponsor isn't willing to own up to the statement if they risk insulting or challenging a higher authority in charge of making those decisions. If you don't work that out in advance, you may have your legs cut out from under you. Picture this scenario: You run and tell Mr. Big that his man on the street tells you that their current program doesn't work. Mr. Big calls your sponsor and barks, "What's this I hear, you disagree with our procedures?" Your sponsor, cornered and in fear of losing his or her livelihood, responds, "Oh no sir, I never said that, that SOB is lying!" It happens all the time. Be sure that your sponsor isn't going to throw you under the bus.

It's best when you can convince your sponsor on the local level to sell it up the chain for you. You must educate your sponsor. He or she must know every aspect of your plan thoroughly enough to sell it on your behalf. Together, brainstorm obstacles that may be presented and ways to overcome them. Ask your sponsor if there are any positive selling features that may help your message hit home. Once uncovered, do some research to find objective evidence that your sponsor can use to support your proposed solution. Your goal is to help him or her be a hero in their company's eyes.

It's not unusual for your sponsor to say, "I'm right there with you, I agree. I just can't get them to go for the idea." Your sponsor may have dozens of agendas that they want their supervisor or HQ to approve, many of which are more important TO THEM than your proposal. They are saying, in essence, "Get in line. I like your proposal, but I have only a few markers and I'm not wasting one on you." Don't fret, it's a natural part of the process. When this happens, thank them for their support and ask if they mind your approaching the decision maker to present your solution. Your sponsor will probably agree since he or she just told you they would do it if it were up to them. Then, and this next step is very important, ask your sponsor, "If I get an audience with the decision maker, can I tell him or her that you saw it and you feel it has merit?" A yes to this question is an important advance. If your sponsor is respected in the organization, an endorsement from him or her is worth many times more than ANYTHING you can say to generate interest in your product or service. If your sponsor is not so well respected than you chose the wrong sponsor.

Take everything you've learned about this customer and go back to the beginning of the READ process. This time, view it from the new decision maker's perspective. This top-to-bottom/bottom-to-top approach is extremely powerful. You stay involved in the process and can steer both ends toward the middle. It's a lot tougher for your sponsor to dismiss your proposal out of hand when they know you have the boss's ear. It's also a lot tougher for the high-level decision maker to blow you off when a respected colleague in the organization has endorsed it.

Small Talk

There is some controversy as to the value of small talk. Proponents of small talk say it builds a personal bond between you and your prospect. That's important since business is about relationships. Opponents say that we are far too busy for idle chatter, and small talk erodes your credibility and wastes your prospect's time. So which is it? Sales is about improving lives and reducing risk. Small talk has value in terms of making the prospect feel more comfortable dealing with you. Finding common ground helps build trust. Trust is essential to alleviate fear of risk. Performed properly, small talk has value. The problem is, too many salespeople do it wrong, and here is the biggest mistake that most salespeople make. They search and search for something in common, however shallow and insignificant it may be. It's great when the thing you have in common is something that has a great deal of importance to your prospect. If you don't have this in common, ask him or her to tell you about what's important to them. You are likely to learn something, not only about the activity but also about your prospect. Once you know more about the activity, you can have that in common with someone else. Wait, it gets even better. Once you learn that someone else is also interested in the same thing (one of your other customers for example), you can mention to your prospect that you met someone you do business with who is also interested. Both people will feel closer to you for having taken the interest, and the testimonial value of coupling your prospect with an existing satisfied customer will have far reaching positive influence.

Before engaging in small talk, think about what your time is worth. Consider also what your prospect's time is worth. When you visit your doctor for a checkup, he or she might engage in a little small talk, but at a couple hundred dollars per hour, how much small talk are you going to get? If your doctor is a specialist, his or her time is worth even more. Small talk in these scenarios is generally outwardly strategic. "What sports do you enjoy?" "What kinds of foods do you eat?" While that can be considered small talk, it gives the doctor clues as to components of your lifestyle that might impact his diagnosis. This is how you must approach small talk in selling. On the first call, a little, and I stress little, small talk helps break the ice. Don't ever lose sight of the fact that, early in the process, you are at best an inconvenience. Excessive small talk will only make your prospect irritable.

Communication Faux Pas

No chapter on communication would be complete if I didn't address a few of my pet peeves. The following phrases should be removed from your vocabulary. They're silent killers. They will erode your effectiveness, and you won't even notice it happening.

"To be honest..."
If you have to clarify that right now you are being honest, you imply that sometimes you are honest and sometimes you are not. Champions are always honest, so they don't have to tell their prospects when they are being so. If you need something to say, try, "To be completely candid..." You might always be honest while occasionally being less that completely candid.

"I can't tell you..."
What you really mean is "I don't know." It may sound like picayune semantics, but it may be impacting your success. Why imply that there is something that you can't say? It may be received as your intention to withhold information or be deceptive.

"I think so..."
It's a watering down phrase you use when you want to make it past the topic at hand without committing. Remember that your objective is to gain a commitment from your prospect to do business with you. How can you expect them to commit when you will not? If you can't provide a solid yes or no, tell them that you will find out and get back to them.

"Probably," "Maybe," "Should be..."

These are also a watering-down statements like, "I think so." They're non-committal. If you say your product will probably perform, don't be surprised when your prospect says they'll probably consider buying it someday. Either a yes or a no is called for in almost every scenario.

"Always," "Never..."

Few things in life can be described in terms of always or never. These are the opposite of watering-down words. They imply a false sense of control over ever-changing circumstances. When you say your product never has a problem or it always works in every situation, your solution will be suspect. Your prospect expects your commitment to do all that you can and to stand behind any problems. Your prospect does not expect perfection.

Religion, politics, bigotry...

Regardless of how comfortable you feel with your prospect, you must stay as far away as possible from the Big 3. These are deeply rooted moral topics that have no place in a business setting. If your prospect tries to engage you in a conversation about any of the above, respectfully decline by saying that they are deeply personal and that you aren't comfortable talking about the issues. It's too great a chance to take.

Profanity...

Lets face it, the rules of business language seem to be getting looser by the day. Even if your prospect enjoys the use of profanity, you're much better off taking the high road. Dropping to his or her level may seem like an opportunity to bond with them and it may be. It may also detract from your credibility. Why take the chance?

9

Driving the Point Home

"We think in generalities but we live in details."
—Alfred North Whitehead

Communicate for Maximum Impact

Once you have a foot in the door, the process of making the prospect your customer has only just begun. You must take full advantage of the opportunity. I'll give you a few real life examples drawn from my career.

Example 1:

I was selling to a very large fleet, we'll call it XYZ Trucking Company. I represented one of the industry's middle tier tire brands, and I was up against my most sophisticated competitor. This was one of the industry's top brands, and I was trying to sell to one of their largest, most important customers. It took months of reconnaissance, examination, and analysis just to be taken seriously. The fleet maintenance management team was charged with the responsibility of determining if there were any products that could lower their overall operating costs. Specific to tires, I was able to learn that there were three primary factors that would impact their decision. The three factors were tire price, how long the tires were going to wear, and how they would impact the fleet's fuel consumption.

As soon as your prospect states that they might consider a test, and not a moment sooner, you must describe the testing methodology that you employ. Using scientific methodology is extremely important in this type of test. Without it, your results will be suspect and can be undone by anyone involved in the decision process who doesn't want you to succeed. Furthermore, by describing a specific process, you will be alleviating unspoken concerns about your proposal. As if you were fishing, you must pay very close attention at this point. If you are getting nibbles, it's time to "set the hook." Here's how.

> ➤ A no-risk guarantee. "If the product doesn't save you money, we'll give you back the difference so that you don't get hurt. You have nothing to lose and so much to gain."
> ➤ A humble commitment to help. Remember, selling is something that you do for your customer, not something that you do to them. There are three possible outcomes. Tell your prospect what they are.
>   1. The product does not perform better than their current supplier, and you credit the difference. You and your prospect learn more about your product and your competitor's product. Your prospect has lost nothing.
>   2. Your product outperforms your competitor's product. It saves your prospect money and they switch to you.

3. Your product outperforms your competitor's product. It saves your prospect money and they use the data to beat your competitor up for a better price. Don't be reluctant to offer this as one of the possible outcomes. If you're selling to a whale, your prospect will think of it anyway. When you offer it verbally, you are saying that you're confident, you are savvy to how the world works and, most importantly, your primary concern is serving the best interests of your clients. You are letting them know that they aren't going to get in a fight with you if they agree to the test and you actually win. Remember that giving your prospect something that they want (a better solution) while giving them something that they don't want (a fight with you) doesn't tip the scales.

Through the test, we determined that our product was wearing 5 percent better. What was especially meaningful, however, was that the trucks running our product showed a 1 percent fuel savings. These types of results highlight the importance of maximizing test results. Unlike the good old days, technology today has closed the gap between the very best and the very worst. Selling is a lot tougher when the differences are that small. While the differences are small, your whales are so big that the small numbers, when calculated out, are dramatic. In this scenario, you are, literally, *Selling by the Numbers*. When dealing with a mega-fleet, a 5 percent increase in tread life is worthwhile. If XYZ has 10,000 trucks each with 10 tires, and my competitor's tires average 150,000 miles and cost $200 each, the prospect will spend about $13,000,000 per year in tires. 5 percent additional tread life equates to a savings of around $650,000. That's probably more than the combined salaries of the three or four people hired by XYZ Company to filter through guys like me. Does 1 percent improvement sound like a great enough incentive to sever a 20-year relationship with their current supplier? One percent doesn't sound like much until you maximize the impact. With 10,000 trucks, traveling an average of 100,000 miles per year operating in the neighborhood of seven miles per gallon and with the cost of fuel at approximately $1.35 per gallon, that's an annual fuel savings of nearly $2,000,000!

Still, had I left my results here, I would not stand a chance. Throughout the test, I worked to get in front of as many people within the organization as possible. I asked each one to recall for me any other competitor that tried to get in. Then I asked what eventually prevented them from succeeding. Only here did I learn what I was really up against. XYZ Trucking hauled freight for many companies. Turns out, not only was my competitor a supplier to XYZ Trucking, they were one of their 10 largest freight customers! These are the tiny little land mines that typically don't get revealed until you're knee deep in the process, well after you get your foot in the door. Timing is everything. First, you have to make them comfortable enough to consider the possibility of doing business with you. Second, you get your foot in the door to prove what you can do and assure them that they stand to lose nothing. You do this by securing a small low-risk or no-risk test. Third, you stay very close during the test. Many salespeople do everything right up until this point. They get the test running, wait until it's near completion then, at the end of the test period, gather the data, summarize it and present it. If it's favorable, they ask for the order. Then when they get a myriad of objections, they stand there defensive and dumbfounded.

With the total picture, I now knew that second position was all I could hope for at this juncture. Fortunately, the fleet was so large that second position was still a lot of business! Offering me second position was a genuine benefit for my customer too. With the impressive performance that my product provided, we kept their primary supplier honest and competitive.

Example 2:

I was selling to a fleet in the south. They hauled specialty gasses including space shuttle fuels. Because they were so specialized, they did not have the same cost pressure as most common carriers. Furthermore, the volatile, sensitive, and dangerous nature of the fuels they hauled shifted their focus to safety at almost any cost. I could not even get an audience with the buyer, as he had been loyal to his current supplier for over 25 years. I learned why no one had been able to steal the business. You couldn't even get in front of him. When I was heading in that direction, I'd call for an appointment. Over the phone, he said in a single sentence, "We're happy with our current supplier; I'll call you if anything changes." Then he hung up. This is an example of the principle of inertia described in chapter 6. I called religiously once per month when I was heading in that direction. I received the same response each time. After a few months, I tried something different. I said, "Mr. Prospect, I'm required to report the status of my top prospects to my boss on a monthly basis. Because you are a premier fleet, you are on my list. I'm embarrassed each month to report that I haven't even met you. Is there any way I can stop by, meet you in the foyer, shake your hand and leave so that I can at least say that I met you?" He chuckled, and gave me the same line, "Like I said, we're happy with our current supplier; I'll call you if anything changes." This guy was tough. As you'll remember from chapter 6, this loyalty is precisely what I look for in a prospect. I was not going to give up. So that I did not become a pest, my next attempt was a thank you letter. It read:

"Thank you for taking my call each month. I know that you're very busy and taking my call must be an interruption of your day. My goal is simple. If I can be of service to you and your organization, I will do all that I

can to help. If I cannot be of service, I will not bother you. You and I are both far too busy to waste our time on insignificant activity. If there is any way, however small, that I can help, please call. As a courtesy, I'll continue to give a quick call whenever I'm heading into your area. If I'm becoming a pest, please let me know."
Thanks!

This is how you differentiate yourself from a competitor. How many sales-people do you think were as persistent? How many do you suppose took the time to write promising to help? How many do you think thanked him for continuing to blow them off? You know the answers, zero, zero, and zero! The next time I called, he agreed to see me. I took the opportunity very seriously. There is a delicate balance. Innately, I felt compelled to give him everything I had for fear that I might not get another chance. That would have been a big mistake. My only goal in this meeting was to prove that I was committed to the long-term nature of the relationship and that I was there to help. Reconnaissance was key. The more I knew without having to ask my prospect the better off I was, especially with a tough prospect like this. I've already hinted how much I cared through my persistence. The purpose of this visit was to cement that message. I did this while asking for a foot in the door. Here's how:

During the meeting, I let him know how impressed I was by his loyalty to his current supplier. I told him how much I appreciated that rare loyalty from several of my customers and told him that if he ever gave me an opportunity, I would never take that loyalty for granted. That's how you plant the seeds. The next time his current supplier takes a little bit longer to return a call, he'll wonder if he's being taken for granted. Then I asked for a foot in the door. I told him that it was my hope to someday be of service. I would be eager to embrace any opportunity to prove what I could do, regardless of difficulty. I thanked him for the time and I left. A month later, on my way to his area, I called. He agreed to meet with me again. This time, he mentioned that there was a tiny little terminal in the northwest out in the middle of nowhere that wasn't getting the service they needed. He asked if I could help. This was it, my opportunity to shine. It turns out that his current supplier felt so confident that they were solidly in control of this business that they just never responded adequately to his complaints about this small outlying terminal.

I jumped on the opportunity with both feet. I'm told that my competitor was relieved that they weren't going to hear him complain about this location any longer. Impressed by my response, he gave me a chance at his next difficult location. I put that high on the priority list and fixed it. Each month, I was given another opportunity, each one better than the last. Within a year and a half, we had all the business. Here's the best part. One of my servicing dealers was talking to my competitor and said, "Shame about you guys losing that account." My competitor responded, "What are you talking about, we didn't lose them." They had taken this account for granted so completely that they did not even notice that they were losing the business! Once they figured it out, they called him for a meeting. What do you think he said? You got it, he told them "We're happy with our current supplier, I'll call you if anything changes." Few things are as troubling as giving someone 100 percent loyalty and having that loyalty taken for granted. He was appalled that they waited that long to respond.

Example 3:

There is a tremendously large fleet that was in my sights. As with the previous examples, they were currently doing business with one of the industry leaders and did not take my company seriously. Over a period of several months, I was able to build a decent relationship with the primary headquarters person. He firmly believed that everything within their control was going as well as could be expected. I asked if it would be okay for me to stop into the branches just to get to know the fleet better in case there ever was an opportunity to help. Notice, I did not say that I was going to look for an opportunity. It may seem like a subtle distinction, but it's important. Looking for an opportunity was self-serving. Getting to know the company in case they needed my help is more altruistic. The response was predictable. He told me, "I have no problem with you stopping in to introduce yourself, but don't try to sell them anything!" I don't want to make this seem easier than it really was. This permission only came after the primary headquarters contact person gained sufficient trust to let me make those visits. Trips to branch locations were initially fruitless, as expected. Like a broken record, each branch manager was defensive and told me that all decisions came from headquarters. What they were really saying was that they didn't want to say anything that might get them into trouble.

I started by asking each branch location operational questions like

- How do you order tires?
- Who do you order them from?
- How do you know what needs to be replaced?
- Who changes them?
- Where do you send the tires that come off?
- Do you have a tire budget?

Like a doctor performing a routine physical, my questions were along the lines of, "Does it hurt when I do this?" After hearing the answers, I went on to another location and asked a similar battery of questions. What I learned was that for every 6 to10 outlying branches, there was a hub location. These hub locations, in effect, filtered the frustration from headquarters. The trouble didn't roll downhill all the way to the branches; it stopped at the hubs. The pain felt by the branches didn't make it all the way back up to HQ since the hubs intercepted it. The hubs were the clearinghouses. They were the ones feeling the pain from both sides. It occurred to me that administering their program involved an awful lot of effort that I could alleviate.

I knew that I was on to something, but I also knew that I didn't have a clear enough picture to start presenting solutions. If I did, I would receive objections. I started getting closer to a few of these hub location managers. I asked them questions regarding what was troubling me about what I saw. I learned that I was not the first person to see these problems. Several before me had attempted to solve their challenges by implementing a tire outsourcing program. Every attempt had failed. I asked several hub managers why these attempts had failed. I learned something that had given me insight, not only into this specific fleet, but into all fleets that operate in that market segment. I learned that outsourcing a tire program left them vulnerable. Outsourcing meant they had to give up more control than they were comfortable giving up. Not outsourcing meant that they needed large staffs of people to administer all the minutia required. Worse yet, their people were freight experts, not tire experts, so the solutions, while in complete control were not necessarily the best solutions.

This was the completion of the reconnaissance and examination phases. I was now moving into the analysis phase. I had confirmation that several within the organization truly wanted to fix this problem. I had the information I needed. Now I simply had to come up with a solution that addressed the problem and the related concerns. I didn't prepare to deliver a single grand presentation. Rather I did enough analysis to deliver a few minor *what-if* scenarios. I presented these what-ifs to several layers up and down the organization to uncover what might still be undiscovered. Each visit brought me closer to full understanding. I came to understand their challenges specific to tires better than any single person in their organization.

This is not a revelation, it's your job! You, as a salesperson and a potential supplier, must know your customer's challenges specific to your product better than any single person in their organization. You can't help if you don't thoroughly understand.

Once the solution was clear and supported through these what-ifs I put together a comprehensive plan to deliver to the hub managers and to headquarters staff. As expected, the concept was well received. I use the word concept because every bold proposal starts as just that. For a concept to become reality it must be put into practice, and that's where the risk comes in. That's why you fight for a foot in the door. I chose a few small branches that appeared to need this solution the most. Since their current program was working so poorly in these locations, there was little risk in giving me a try. With this foot in the door, I was able to show that the concept actually works! There was another real benefit. With a small foot in the door at a trouble location, I had a chance to work any minor bugs out of the program without them being aware. Trying to beta test in a high volume key location is a scary place to start. If there are any bugs, they'll blow out of proportion fast rapidly taking the luster off your program.

I didn't even have to ask for more locations. They were so thrilled with my performance that they were calling me to take on more locations. Somewhere after the twentieth location, I was asked to summarize this program and burn it onto a CD-ROM so that they could distribute it throughout their organization. It became their internal platform for outsourcing.

There was another amazing benefit. It wasn't until a week after they agreed to let me take over the first location that someone in purchasing asked, "What are the prices for these services?" That's how you know you did it right. When your prospect is so convinced that you can solve a problem that price becomes an afterthought!

Micro or Macro, Which Comes First?

Notice a common thread in each of the above scenarios. The foot-in-the-door was simply an opportunity to showcase my capabilities on a small or micro scale. There was little or no broad risk for my prospect. Once established, I multiplied the benefit from that micro across the overall program to the macro. I was, in essence, saying, "Here's your savings per truck times this many trucks. That will net an overall savings of this much." When you're communicating savings for maximum impact, you always go from micro to macro.

Conversely, if I were faced with communicating cost, such as a new computer system serving the entire organization nationwide or worldwide, I would go in reverse from macro to micro. "The total cost is this, which amounts to only this much per location, per employee, per truck, and so forth." When helping your prospect to understand the value, it is critically important that you portray the benefits in as large a scale as possible while illustrating the costs in small numbers.

Your Humble Servant

The common thread in each of the above examples is humility. Each started with a foot in the door and a sincere desire to uncover problems and provide solutions. I've seen arrogance kill more opportunities than any single personality trait. It's killed more opportunity than insecurity, insincerity, or inconsistency. Arrogance is more destructive than lack of knowledge, lack of skill, or lack of experience. Arrogant salespeople go into selling situations asking, "What's in it for me?" When presented with the toughest, ugliest, littlest opportunity, they get insulted. They develop an attitude that implies. "If I do that for you, what will you do for me?" In essence, they are displaying the same selfish posture as the current supplier who is taking the client for granted. That's why it doesn't work. The scales never tip.

Regardless of data, business is about relationships. The foot in the door that you secured is your opportunity to build the relationship. Once a test is running, you're no longer a predator, you're a supplier. You're on the inside. You have a greater opportunity to learn what makes your prospect tick from the inside. Done properly, by the time the test is complete, there is no more selling to do. Instead of kicking into selling mode at the end of the test, you must use your new inside position to continue moving toward your objective. Find out what other factors, departments, or individuals influence the decision. As a supplier, you will be allowed access to more people within the organization than you had as a solicitor. Your objective in this crucial step is to exhume any problems that your competitor has buried or overlooked. You must outshine your competitor. If you still have a lot of selling to do at the end, you've messed up.

The test gave your prospect a glimpse of what it will be like doing business with you. Even if they like what they see, they may have to sell it to their boss, their stockholders, their board, or their department heads, or whomever. That's why you document and maximize the test results. The data is the rationalization they need to justify the decision to himself or herself and to everyone else. From example 1, when they are in front of their people describing what they refer to as a 1 percent savings, they may meet resistance. When they present a potential $2,650,000 savings, they'll get their listeners' attention. In examples 2 and 3 you want to show some kind of before and after snapshots of what you had achieved. Your proposal must include all of the downsides of your product or service. This is counterintuitive for most salespeople. You may be thinking that they can come up with enough of their own reasons for not doing business with you, so why would you give them any more? Remember, with a whale, you are not only selling the concept to your contact, he or she is going to have to sell it to others within their organization that you may not even meet. The people that they are presenting to may have objections that your sponsor had not thought of. So that you don't "throw them under the bus," you must think of those obstacles for them and make sure they are prepared to address them, or you both will lose. When the hidden objective is a sensitive issue like business reciprocity, as in example 1, you don't want to put it in writing.

If you've done everything right thus far, your contact wants to do business with you and has the needed justification to rationalize the decision. Be absolutely certain that your case for change is honest and that the results are sound. If the data you present to your contact is flawed and the flaws are revealed while your contact is trying to sell it to someone else, you're in serious trouble. Your credibility will be shot, and your opportunity will disappear!

One additional word on humility:

Always deliver a little something more than you promise. Make sure your customer knows that you gave them a small bonus as a token of your appreciation for their business. That's one more reason why you always hold something back when bidding on the business.

The Yin and the Yang of the Selling Process.

"Within your greatest weaknesses lie your greatest strengths."—Chinese Proverb

We tend to think of good and bad as being at opposite ends of a spectrum and that everything falls somewhere along the line.

GOOD ⟷ BAD

In reality, nothing in life can be categorized as strictly good or bad. What is good can be bad. What is bad can be good. Earlier, I cited an example of selling a home. If the home is located in a far suburb, the distance from the congestion of the city may be a tremendous benefit to a retiree. That very same distance may be a real deterrence to someone who has to commute into the city every day for work. Relationships also work this way. When choosing a mate, one person may seek stability and dependability while another may seek the opposite hoping to find excitement and spontaneity. As you dig deep, here's what you'll find. Anything that is a minor advantage to one is likely to be a minor disadvantage to another. If something is a major advantage to one, it's probably a major disadvantage to another. In business, the size of your organization can be one of these items. If you are a very large, multi-state supplier, you will appeal to large prospects needing program consistency. If you are a small local vendor, you will appeal to the entrepreneur who does not want to be just another number.

Too many salespeople and too many companies ignore this as they try to keep from alienating anybody. They make it a point to not stray very far from the center. The problem with staying in the middle of the road is that it's the place where you're most likely to get run over! It's the principle of differentiation that I've addressed throughout this book. In order for your offering to be appealing, it must include some unique and robust differences. Those differences must be real and they must set you apart from your competition. If they are significant, they will actually make you less appealing to some other buyers. As the old expression goes, "One man's ceiling is another man's floor." The worst thing you can do is to neutralize or water down those differences. While you might make your proposal less troubling, it will also be less intriguing.

Here's one of those pearls that can make a rapid and significant improvement in your effectiveness. Think in terms of the apothecary scale illustrated earlier. Visualize stacking dozens of tiny little features onto the scale in hopes of tipping the sale in your favor. As you do this, your prospect may consider some features beneficial and place them in the tray on the left. They may, however, consider the feature to be a disadvantage and place that feature in the tray on the right. You keep dropping these little benefits hoping that it tips in your favor. What happens is that the scale teeters gently back and forth. You never make a clear and compelling case, and your prospect, stuck in inertia, tells you that they still don't see a reason to make change. If they're kind, they'll probably say that they have to think about it. What they may be saying is that you have provided so many little features that they haven't determined which are good, which are bad, and which don't matter. Furthermore, once they've determined which are good or bad, they may need to think how heavy each individual feature is. The score may be three in favor, one opposed. If the combined weight of each favorable component cannot outweigh the one primary opposed component, you have a problem. If it's close, you'll have procrastination.

The first thing you must do is to stop talking in terms of just good or bad, but also in terms of major or minor. More importantly, you must be clear whether they are good, bad, major, or minor specific to each prospect. That's what this process is about. That's why you must first learn what makes your prospect tick prior to providing features and benefits; otherwise, your benefit might be used against you!

Have you ever identified one or more dramatic differentiators, tried to use them and been shot down? If you tell someone that you're the top selling salesperson in your organization, they may feel like you're well suited to help, or they might feel they're not going to get personal attention. Tell them that you're just starting to build your territory and they might feel like you'll work hard to take good care of them, or they might feel like you don't have enough experience to handle their challenges. Tell someone you've been in the profession for over 25 years (like me for example), and your prospects might feel like your experience will be of great benefit to them or they might be afraid that you're out of touch with the latest developments. I could go on, but I think you get the point. Any single motivating factor is never JUST good or bad. It will be good or bad, major or minor depending upon the circumstances.

In ancient Chinese philosophy, the Yin and the Yang refer to equal and opposite forces that govern behavior. The Yin is a dark, negative pessimistic force, the Yang, a bright, positive optimistic force. Think about that while taking a close look at the Yin and Yang symbol above.

Notice first, that they form a continuous circle. Remember that what is a strength will also be a weakness and what is a weakness can also be strength. Weak mediocre strengths and weak mediocre weaknesses don't tip the scales. Only bold differentiators tip the scales. Let me give you an example.

I worked for a manufacturer that was recovering from an era of product performance problems. Eight to ten years ago, the industry was going through a tough period of consolidations. This company, at the time, was highly diversified. The product line I was charged with selling was in a mature and highly competitive segment. Consequently, profit margins were very tight. Since other divisions in this conglomerate were much more profitable and had greater growth potential, they were the ones to get most of the capital. No one wanted to sink money into this flat and struggling division. Product innovation and quality suffered. Finally, this division was spun off to a foreign company. Even though the product was dramatically superior following the buyout, nearly every prospect I stopped in to see chased me out either because they actually owned one of these problem products in the past or knew someone who did. It became pretty frustrating. When I told them whom I represented, I was told, in essence, "Thanks but no thanks." Occasionally someone would be generous enough to tell me why he or she had no use for me. More often than not, they would simply say, "I'm happy with my present supplier."

Then I did something out of pure desperation. I wish I could tell you that I was taught how to do this. It would have been a lot quicker if I had been. No, I learned this principle the hard way and purely by luck born of frustration. I had to try something new or I was going to stop trying altogether. Rather than watering down the significance of our company's past problems, I flipped the negative differentiator into a positive. The results were astonishing. Here's how it worked.

I would stop in, introduce myself and tell my prospect who I represented. At the first sign of resistance, I would say, "Let me guess, you used my company's product about 8 to10 years ago. Am I right?" Wow! Instantly the conversation turned. The response was typically, "Yeah I did, and I swore I'd never buy it again!" To which I responded, "It probably doesn't surprise you that I get a lot of that; it's the single most common hurdle I have to deal with." The conversation would continue in a positive tone because we already had something in common. We agreed that the product my company used to sell was total garbage! Here's the next step, and it must be sincere. I would say, "The funny thing is, that's exactly the reason why you should seriously consider buying it today." I have never failed to get my prospect intrigued with that comment. Usually the prospect would say, in a sarcastic tone, "And why is that?" Now I've got them. I have been invited to differentiate myself. I was no longer at arms' length hearing, "Thanks, we're happy with our current supplier."

Here I employed what I later learned to be the principle of the Yin and the Yang, making the greatest negative into the greatest positive attribute of my product. I would explain that if my company today built the same quality product that they built back then, they would be out of business, and I would not be here trying to sell it. Because there were so many problems, the company was suffering and, consequently, was a great takeover opportunity for a large European company that wanted to gain a foothold in the United States. Then I would describe what this new European parent company brought to the mix. I went on to say, "We knew that even a single small problem would be interpreted by our customers as "Here we go again, same old stuff!" Because of that oversensitivity, we have to make sure that not a single unit leaves the plant that isn't absolutely perfect. We are the only manufacturer in the industry that x-rays every single unit before it leaves the plant. While our competitor can get away with a little problem here or there, we can't, don't you agree?" But, like an infomercial, don't answer yet, there's more. I went on to say, "Also, my competitor can charge more for their product because they don't have a bad reputation to dig out of. People will simply not pay as much for my product. Which means that if you buy from me, you are getting a product that has to be as good or better than any in the industry. And it will be at a more competitive price. Higher quality and lower price is the definition of value, and isn't value what it's all about when making a purchase of this nature?" I went on to say, "In addition, each person in our organization is totally committed to returning this company to its former glory as one of the founders of the industry. In so doing, you will not find anyone who is not totally committed to your complete satisfaction. Can you say that about your present supplier?"

The hardest part of the selling process is convincing your prospect that you are different. In this scenario, you won't have to do much work to convince them that you're different. They already told you that. All you have to do is convince them that the difference is actually a good thing, not a bad thing. Once you get the hang of it, it's much easier than you think. It works so well that you'll actually hope they had a problem with your product in the past.

There's another powerful way to use this principle. We spoke earlier about complimenting your competitor. When your prospect begins to tell you what your competitor does well, he or she is opening the door for use of this principle. Instinctually, salespeople try to overcome or offset their competitor's strengths. While it works, it's not nearly as effective as flipping a strength into a weakness. Remember, through the principle of the Yin and the Yang, every strength can be weakness, and every weakness can be strength. As you picture the scale, visualize taking a block off of the negative tray and placing it onto the positive tray. That will have twice as powerful an effect as just dropping an additional block onto a tray.

Yin and Yang play a major role in your prospect selection process as well. For example, is having a large number of small prospects good or bad? It's good because you don't have all your eggs in one basket, so no single account is in a position to devastate your territory. It's bad because it's much tougher to achieve customer intimacy with a large number of clients than with a small number, so each account is more vulnerable. Is working in a major metropolitan area good or bad? It's typically good because there are many more prospects to call on. It's bad because you have more competitors calling on them. This list can go on ad infinitum.

Getting in to See the Tough Customer

"Nobody Gets in to See the Wizard, Not Nobody Not No How!"—The Wizard of Oz

I'm frequently asked whether a salesperson should call for an appointment or just stop in. Sometimes, if you just stop in, your prospect will become irritated that you did not call for an appointment. Conversely, sometimes when you call for an appointment, you get blocked by the screening secretary or receptionist and never get a return call. There is no one right answer to this question, which is why it's so daunting.

On the first cold call, make the visit in person by just strolling in. You have this one chance to claim ignorance and say that you just didn't know any better. If the receptionist says, "He or she prefers to work by appointment, but let me see if they can meet with you," you'll know that an appointment is recommended but not required. If you encounter a brick wall and hear something like, "He or she sees no one without an appointment," ask the receptionist his or her name and thank him or her. Ask if you can schedule an appointment right there. I've had it happen. Otherwise, get the number and call back. One word of caution: on several occasions, I've left the receptionist, gone out to my car and called for an appointment. I've learned the hard way that it's a bad idea. I can't really explain why, but it seems to come across as pushy and sneaky. Wait until the next day before calling to schedule. It works much better.

There are cases where the receptionist makes it clear that you cannot and will not see your prospect without an appointment. If you call for an appointment and can't get through to the buyer, here are a few tips about leaving messages.

> ➤ Never leave more than one message per week. Your prospect may be on vacation or assigned to a special project or task. If he or she is checking their messages and have two or three from you in the same week it will turn them off.

> ➤ Leave your number, but don't expect them to call you back. If a receptionist is taking the message, just leave your name, your company name, and a phone number, nothing more. If you're sent to voicemail, your message should sound something like this, "Good morning, my name is Jason Miller, I'm a representative for ABC Company. I would love an opportunity to speak briefly with you. If you have a moment to talk, I can be reached at…. I'm sure you're busy as we all are these days; if I don't hear from you, I'll try back next week. Thanks." Then, if you don't hear back, call as promised. You do this for two important reasons. When you tell them to call you back, you are adding items to

their to-do list. You are not in a position to assign them work. They're the boss, not you. Secondly, by letting them know you'll call back, you let them know that you are persistent and that this is more than a casual visit, so they have an added incentive to go ahead and call since you're probably not going to go away until they do.

➢ DO NOT leave a number to your voicemail or pager. Ideally, you can leave a message to a cell phone that you always have with you. If you have an assistant or a secretary, that's another great number to leave. Be sure to tell your assistant or secretary that you're expecting this person's call. Instruct them to say, "Yes, he was expecting your call. I'm sorry, but he has stepped out briefly. He'll be disappointed that he missed the call. What would be a good time to have him return the call?" What you're trying to avoid is telephone tag. Once your prospect has returned your call, your follow-up calls should not request a return call. If you call and miss, explain that you seem to be playing phone tag and that you'll keep trying. If that's not successful, make sure your messages include a time frame for when it is easiest to reach you.

➢ In the cases where you've left more than three messages and have not received a return call, try a letter. Letters work well because they can be opened and read at your prospect's convenience. The added effort proves that you're professional and that you're serious. It differentiates you from your competition.

Thank-You Cards

No single form of communication is as consistently powerful as a handwritten thank-you note. Yet hardly anyone uses them. Just the mere fact that you took the time will differentiate you from your competition. Because they're hand-written, they help build relationships by adding a personal touch. And they're real. You should feel grateful that your prospect has taken time out of his or her busy schedule to visit with you. Your prospect will say, perhaps out loud, "It's about time someone took the opportunity to appreciate me!"

If you want what may be the only quick fix presented in this book, it's this. Start using handwritten thank-you notes. You will see instant results.

10

The Learning Curve

"While you're green, you're growing.
Once you're ripe, you begin to rot."
—*Anonymous*

Being All That You Can Be

"The only way to find the limits of the possible is by going beyond them to the impossible."—Arthur Clarke

This book was written for salespeople, not for sales managers. In the very first chapter, I talked about the many wrong ways to approach a career in selling. I listed them so that you can be aware of any sales manager who tries to coach you with one of these tired, worn-out approaches. The reality is, you're on your own. If you are to realize all of your potential, you're going to have to take responsibility for your own success. If you're not currently realizing your full potential, determining who to blame is unimportant. Since the scenery only changes for the lead dog, the only thing that matters is that you become totally committed to reaching your full potential right here and right now. You can be a leader!

Do all salespeople have the same potential? No, they don't! Everyone who enters a career in selling brings with them early programming that will dramatically impact where they peak out. Factors limiting potential include the following.

➢ Fear:
   o You may be intimidated by larger accounts. Throughout this book, you should have picked up the message that you will need to migrate you account base to larger accounts if you intend to grow your hourly wage and reach your goals.
   o You may not be able to get yourself to de-emphasize those smaller accounts that sap your time and energy. If this is the case, you're just afraid of losing your current base and moving down Maslow's pyramid as described in chapter 2.
   o Then there's the proverbial old dog afraid of new tricks: The world simply does not stand still. If you're afraid to abandon the mediocre methods that got you this far, you will not realize the benefit of newer more effective methods needed to succeed in today's environment.
➢ Starting point: I have developed a passion for hiking. Several friends and I recently climbed to the peak of Mt. Charleston just outside of Las Vegas. At just under 12,000-foot elevation, it was a terrific hike. How great an accomplishment it was depends on several factors, not the least of which was the elevation at the trailhead. Had we started at 10,000 feet it would have been a lot easier than starting down at 7,000 feet. It's much the same concept when discussing the learning curve.

Reaching a higher level of performance is a whole lot easier if you're building upon an existing competency. Mediocre salespeople go through the curve, and once they've made it through, breathe a sigh of relief and hold their ground. If this is you, whatever level of potential you are on track for will become fixed as your lifelong maximum. If, as a lifelong learner, you enjoy any height of success just long enough to catch your breath and climb on, you potential may be limitless. Top performers view the learning curve as nothing more than a snapshot. Once they make it through to the current level of success, they start looking toward their next curve. Any opportunity to grow is evaluated and seriously considered. The fact that you are reading this book indicates that you are either at the beginning of your first learning curve or evaluating your next growth opportunity. The more you learn, the more you'll realize how little you know. If you take this approach to life, you will constantly be embarking on new and greater learning curves while constantly achieving greater levels of personal success.

➤ Belief: Salespeople will be successful only to the extent that they truly believe they are capable and no more. Deeply rooted in the subconscious, people are incapable of performing at a level beyond what they believe is possible. As Henry Ford said, "Whether you believe that you can or that you cannot, you're probably right!" Your peers will influence some of this. If you are already the top performer in your organization, it may take a lot to convince yourself that you can "boldly go where no man has gone before." If you are not the top salesperson in your industry, you only need convince yourself that you are equally worthy of that distinction. Suppress the negative self-talk and lose the excuses and rationalizations.

➤ Motivation, drive: Some salespeople have an intrinsically high achievement orientation. If this is you, skip forward to the next section. If this is not you, go back and complete the goal-setting exercise earlier in this book. Whether your motivation is innate or deliberate, reaching a high level of performance requires a burning desire to leap out of bed each morning and greet the challenges you will encounter.

➤ Commitment, sheer determination: No single factor will more directly influence your potential than your level of commitment. Call it self-discipline, determination, or whatever you're most comfortable calling it. It's all the same thing. In the truest terms, when the going gets tough, the tough get going.

> ➢ Lack of training, coaching, mentoring, or support during the most critical phase in the learning curve: This also applies to training provided too early or too late in the curve. Learning is only one side of the equation. If you're going to learn, someone or something has to teach. If you're blessed to be working under a gifted teacher, you're in the minority. If you don't have a teacher readily available, you may have to find one. There are many options. You might consider night classes, books, seminars, audiocassettes, peers, magazines, friends, and relatives. The potential you will realize depends upon your having access to the training that you will need.

Work the Curve or Let It Work You—the Choice Is Yours

There is a very specific process that every salesperson must go through in order to get from zero to their full potential. How you make it through will create the mold that will inevitably shape your career. You must understand the process if you hope to navigate it effectively.

The journey from zero to your full potential will take you through four distinct phases. Each point along the way can be defined in terms of two components. The first component is knowledge. At the beginning of your career, you have very little of the knowledge you'll need to be successful. With each day and each experience comes a piece of knowledge that will help you get the job done. The importance of knowledge is fairly self-explanatory. The second component is awareness. Simple, yet a little bit more involved than knowledge. When you're brand new, you aren't even aware of what you'll need to know. It isn't until your customers and prospective customers ask questions that you cannot answer that you become aware of what you need to learn. Paradoxically, at some point in a salesman's career, they may reach a level of experience where they have an intuitive awareness of the business and they somehow come up with the right answers without even having to think about it. When asked how they did it, they are often hard-pressed to give much more explanation than "it just seemed like the right thing to do." And it was. In other words, they aren't even aware of how much they know. How's that for kick. In the beginning, you're not aware of how much you don't know, and later you're not aware of how much you actually do know.

You'll see these two components illustrated in the chart. Knowledge continues to increase through the curve and through your career. Awareness, on the other hand, tends to increase to a point and then decrease for the reasons I just described. Many notable authors and psychologists have segregated this process into four distinct phases. Each phase has unique attributes and needs. The better you understand these phases, the more prepared you will be to take the necessary steps to move through the process and move toward your goals.

The first phase I call *The Rookie*. Rookies come into the job loaded with enthusiasm. And why shouldn't they? Everyone has seen a salesperson in action somewhere and thinks, "How hard could that be?" So they jump in reaching for the stars in hopes of making a name for themselves. Being a rookie is an exciting time since the future looks so bright. Many experts call the salesperson during this phase the *unconscious incompetent* since he or she doesn't know but doesn't know that he doesn't know.

Phase two I call the *Trained Salesperson*. By the time they reach phase two, these salespeople have picked up enough knowledge to develop an awareness of the position. With this awareness comes the stark reality that it's not as easy as it looks. In phase two, the giddy enthusiasm begins to fade as it is replaced by concern and frustration. They've been tenderized, beaten up and lightly seasoned a few times by customers and competitors. Reality sets in as they begin to wonder what they got themselves in to. Phase two is a critical phase. If you give up easily, phase two will knock you out of a career in sales. The experts refer to phase two as the *conscious incompetent*. The phase two sales-person still doesn't know, but they now know what they don't know.

Phase three may define the overall quality of your career. If you've made it through phase two, you're probably capable of surviving as a career salesper-son. I call phase three the *Experienced salesperson*. Somewhere in phase three is where a salesperson generates enough revenue to pay for themselves. By phase three you've paid your dues and, if you have only moderate ambition, you're probably closing in on your comfort zone. Over 90 percent of the career sales-people that I've worked with land here, stall out, take a sigh of relief as they make it out of the woods, and coast. Experts refer to phase three as the *conscious competent*. This is someone who knows what they're doing and knows that they know.

Phase four, the *seasoned pro* is an amazing place that only a select few will ever experience. It's a shame really since the payoff is much greater compared to the effort and energy required. Phase four, as the diagram illustrates, is where the expression "It's all downhill from here" comes from. It's the rarified air that Paredo referred to in his 80/20 rule. If you make it into phase four, you'll write your own ticket. Phase four salespeople can work anywhere they want because companies need them even more than these salespeople need their employers. Phase four salespeople have the ultimate job security stem-ming from the knowledge that if their current employer lets them down, they can find another job overnight. Phase four salespeople are recession proof. When tough economic times hit, companies reduce expenses. Since phase four salespeople are strong revenue generators, companies will never lay them off! Experts refer to phase four as the *unconscious competent* since they may not even know how much they know.

It's Never Too Late For a Fresh Start

"The best time to plant a tree was 20 years ago. The second best time is now."
—Chinese Proverb

Here's some good news. You're never stuck in your current level of perform-ance just because you've completed the learning curve. The learning curve and the learning process also apply to revitalizing a stagnant career. You may have a phase four grasp on the skill set needed for your current level of performance. If you want your career to grow, however, you must learn and grow. If you want to hike a mountain, climbing to 12,000 feet elevation is a whole lot easier when you start at 6,000 feet than it would be starting at sea level. If you're a lifelong learner, you'll have a lifetime of growth. Becoming a champion is an evolution not a revolution, and all successful salespeople will inevitably go through these four basic phases of development at least once during their career. Real champions go through some form of this process many times. In fact, they never completely stop going through. Going through the second time is bound to be a little bit scary. You'll need to knock yourself back to phase two where you were more receptive to training and learning. On the pages that follow, I have outlined each stage and illustrated the way it's typically done. I've illustrated the wrong way and the preferred way.

Are We There Yet?

There is no hard and fast rule regarding how long you should expect each phase to take. The more ambitious your goals are, the longer it will take to master the skills you'll need. If you're a fast learner, you will complete the process in less time. That being said, here are a few rules of thumb:

Phase one is the most consistent of the four phases. There aren't any short-cuts. It's unlikely that you will enjoy phase one bliss for longer than a couple of months. Still, you probably won't internalize your most critical development needs in fewer than five or six months.

Phase two is the Darwinian, survival of the fittest, moment of truth. Many salespeople get a couple of weeks into phase two and, learning that it's tougher than they thought, give up. The rest manage to muster up the discipline and courage to forge ahead. Assuming you aren't one of the casualties, expect it to take six months to a year for you to reach the level of competence needed to promote to phase three. You can speed up phase two by taking a proactive approach to training. Read books, attend seminars, listen to educational audio cassettes, ask your sales manager and your higher performing peers to work with you and give you tips.

Phase three is a different story altogether. Since only the champions ever really make it through phase three to the other side, for most salespeople it's forever and that's a shame. A salesperson's life doesn't really get exciting until phase four. In three, it's still a lot like work.

Phase four is that special place reserved for the select few top performers. Once admitted, you're pretty well guaranteed membership for life. Life as a salesperson in phase four is pretty special. The most aggressive salespeople in this phase will use their new starting point and work up from there in order to secure even higher levels of performance. They become the TOP OF THE TOP.

These salespeople typically earn more than their boss! Then there are the legends. These are the ones who continue to strive and become the best-of-the-best. They operate in the top 1 percent of all salespeople and may be the highest paid people in their organizations.

Phase One through Four Action Steps

Typical Rookie (Stage 1)

Typically in stage 1, management inundates a new salesperson with more training than he or she can possibly absorb. New salespeople are hard-pressed to separate the crucial information from the less crucial. Remember that in phase one, you don't yet know what you need to learn. Having no idea what they need to know, they remember some of the less important training, forget some of the more important training, and confuse it all. With no experience, rookies have no practical application for what they learn, so it becomes little more than a bunch of words. Furthermore, rookies often miss the opportunity to relearn the material at a later time when it will have more value. As they spend time in training, they waste time that they could have used in front of potential customers finding out what they need to learn as they move forward toward phase two. Keeping rookies in training until they're ready is like saying, "Don't go near the water until you learn to swim!"

Preferred Rookie

A better approach is to commit a smaller block of time to training primarily to keep them from doing any damage, a larger block of time planning, and the majority of their time cold calling on prospective customers. Being in front of potential customers is the only way a new salesperson will determine what they need to learn. In the process they will develop a feel for the competition, the potential, the marketplace and the job skills they'll need to learn. He or she will learn how to get around efficiently and what the marketplace's perception of their company is. These are all traits present in sales champions that can't be effectively taught in a classroom. These traits must be learned firsthand.

As a bonus, in the process, the rookie will filter through the potential customers and learn more about them. Later, when he or she is ready to focus on serious solicitation, they'll know where to go that might have need of what they're selling. The more prospects they meet, the more likely they are to develop a strong standby list.

Typical Trained Salesperson (Phase 2)
Typically in stage 2, the salesperson now has his or her feet wet, and the training falls way off. The thought from management is: "We've done our job training this person early in their career. He or she now needs to hit the streets and pay for himself or herself." Planning, for most, is on its way off the to-do list. Many managers feel that the only profitable time is that which is spent in front of a customer, any customer.

This is a pivotal point in the careers of most salespeople. Salespeople now know what they don't know and realize that the job is a little bit tougher than it looks. They become frustrated.

Preferred Trained Salesperson
This is a critical time when they now know what they don't know. Without intensive training at this point, finding the answers is left to trial and error. They may get lucky and find the right method. They may eek out acceptable but not ideal solutions, or they may get frustrated and quit. Disillusionment is forthcoming.

As much time as possible should be spent in training. Ideally, the salesperson will bring the pro into the tough prospects that he or she smoked out in phase one. Training means so much when a salesperson can see how it's done in a real-life situation. Planning must continue to be strong. It's one of those critical disciplines that is so easy to abandon once the territory starts cooking.

When you find yourself in phase two, what's most important is that you just stick with it and learn as much as you can.

Typical Experienced Salesperson (Phase 3)
For those that make it to stage 3, the path is usually set. While few make it here, fewer still make it with all the excitement and passion they had when they started. It's a decent job, but the "Emerald City" now seems like a vague and distant dream. Time to prospect is dramatically diminished due to demands from existing customers and administration. Prospecting is tougher since you've landed those accounts that were most receptive to you and least loyal to your competitor.

Juggling all the demands of a territory that is up and running consumes planning time, and training all but disappears.

Preferred Experienced Salesperson
In these turbulent times, you may have to plan on replacing as much as 15 to 20 percent of your business each year just to stay even! You were also challenged to factor in your personal income goal, cost of living increases, and more.

What you'll find is that considerably more time is needed in prospecting efforts if you are to reach your goals. Training must be ongoing. At least once per year, each of us must be reminded of the basics. It's easy to get rusty. Planning should be vigorous and consistent to make the most of your precious time. Since an experienced salesperson has many more urgencies to juggle, "If they fail to plan, they are planning to fail!"

If you follow the account migration steps outlined in this book, you'll have less time dominated by your existing customers, freeing up precious time for these other critical activities.

Typical Seasoned Professional (Phase 4)

If you make it, this will be the most exciting phase in your career. One can only hope that by now everything else has taken place correctly. Habits are now deeply engrained, and they are very difficult to change. Existing customers now consume all of your time, training seems pointless, and planning seems unnecessary. You know what needs to be done without giving it much thought; it's relatively "automatic." Administration is a bear, but as a seasoned pro, no one much challenges you regarding how much time you spend in the office. If this is you, the mere fact that you're reading this book and have made it this far indicates that you are open to change. If quantum change is what you're seeking, it's going to be more work than you expect.

Preferred Seasoned Professional

I'm recommending the same ratio of time spent reflected in stage 3. For one thing, the fact that you are a seasoned pro should not preclude ongoing training. We live in a life of rapid change. Today, more than ever, we need to find the time to stay current and focused. Also, as with stage 3, annual refreshers are critical. While existing customers will still consume most of your time, a seasoned pro should be able to handle more in less time. Effectively doing that may require even more planning than in earlier stages! Prospecting is essential. With more business in hand, there's much more to lose.

Hands-down, the greatest challenge facing seasoned pros is their own comfort zone. They feel they've paid their dues, and they're content. It's a shame really since these people have a greater chance of real sales growth than salespeople in any of the previous stages.

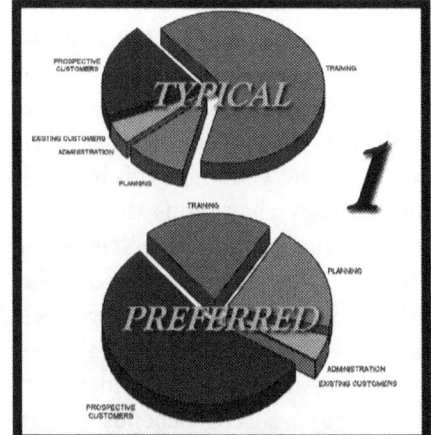

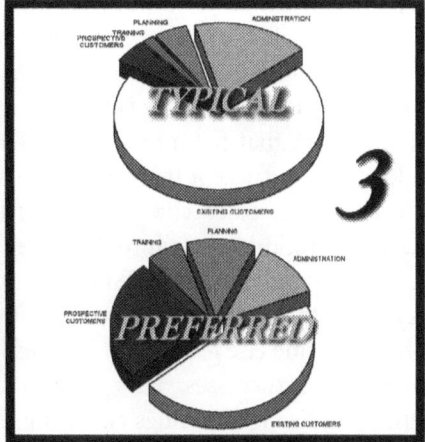

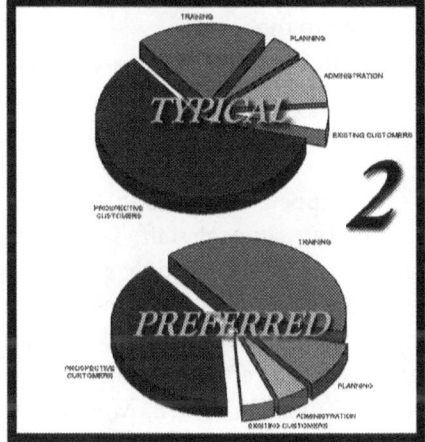

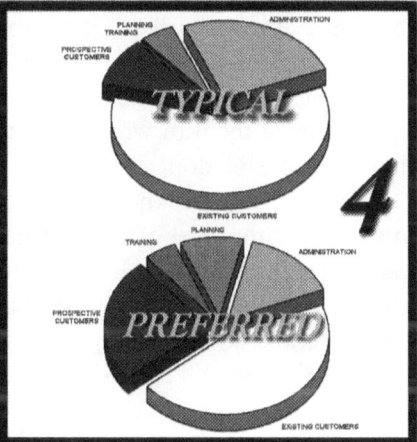

Commitment

"Do or do not, there is no 'try.'"—Yoda (Star Wars)

We've discussed deciding precisely what you want. We've begun to address how you're going to get it. There is one critical last step. If you do nothing else, this one step separates champions from their peers. You must completely remove the word *try* from your vocabulary. Commitment is the adhesive that holds your activity to your goals. Without commitment, your goals become little more than dreams you once had. If your goals are ambitious and worthwhile, they won't come easy; nothing worthwhile ever does. Commitment is the driving force that helps you blast through or finds a detour around the obstacles you are sure to encounter along the way. Most average salespeople can tell you all of the obstacles that they encountered on the road to success. As they *try* to convince you that failure was not their fault, they assume that everyone will understand and accept their mediocre results. By now, you know this is simple rationalization. Sales champions don't do it. Sales champions don't make excuses or rationalize failure. Whether or not someone else understands and accepts their failure is of little importance to them. Sales champions know what they want, they know why they want it and they intend to achieve it regardless of how any one else feels about it. Sales champions believe that they are the reason for their successes. They know that if you assign blame to someone or something else when things go wrong, then failure OR success depends on outside forces. Champions are not quick to give credit away to anyone or anything else. Sales champions believe "If it is to be, it is up to me."

Once you've made a commitment to yourself, you must make a commitment to your organization. No excuses. If you said you were going to bring in the sales, bring them in whatever it takes. If your original prospect list isn't going to get the job done, revise it.

When you become known as a "make it happen" salesperson, you can demand the same level of commitment from your support staff. This won't come overnight. Once you have committed to your goals, schedule a meeting with your manager and/or your support staff. Sit down with them, away from distractions and lay out what you are going to do. If you use words like "What I plan to do," "What I'll try to do," or "What I'm going to attempt," don't be surprised if you get the same half-hearted commitment in return. Most likely, your response will be something like "That's great, IF you do that we SHOULD be able to support it." Or "We'll sure TRY our best!" You must become keenly aware of the use of water-down words like *if, should, attempt, maybe, likely, probably,* the ever popular *I think so,* or my personal favorite, *I'll try.* Anytime you hear these words what you are really hearing is *Don't count on it.* The only reason you use these words is to imply a chance of success while convinced of the likelihood of failure!

Selling by the Numbers is designed to eliminate any chance of failure. If your organization is not prepared to support a full-scale effort on your part, you will fail. If your manager or support team uses water-down words, they are telling you that they are already preparing for failure.

What you need to hear is a definite, concrete commitment. This is how it should sound; "WHEN you bring in the business, we WILL handle it." Short of that is conversation, not commitment.

The difference between conversation and commitment

Instead of...	You need to hear...
Maybe, probably, likely	Definitely, absolutely
Try, attempt	Will
Should, might	Will

Too many salespeople want to put the cart before the horse. You'll hear them say things like "*If* my company were committed to supporting my effort, *then* I would go get more business." Whether or not they choose to admit it, these are lame excuses. Ask yourself if you are truly committed to the goals you created previously. If your answer sounds anything like "I think so," "Probably" or "I'll try," save yourself the aggravation, you've already failed. If your response was *"Absolutely and nothing but nothing is going to stop me!"* you will succeed regardless of whether or not you finish this book or choose to do it my way. There is no pride in achieving easy goals, especially if you succeeded because of luck. Deep inner pride of accomplishment comes from the successful realization of worthy goals. The tougher the journey was, the more pride you'll feel when you get there.

I'll give you an example of commitment from my own life. Several years ago, I was struggling to come up with a motivational presentation to my sales staff about the power of commitment. While pondering my approach, it quietly occurred to me that, at 70 pounds overweight, I might have had some difficulty selling a message on commitment. Then it hit me: I was in a perfect position to demonstrate the power of commitment. I stood in front of my team, and here's what I said. "To illustrate the power of commitment, I will bet anyone in this room any amount that they are willing to lose that within one year from today I will weigh less than 200 pounds. Nothing but nothing is going to stop me!" Then I asked, "Are there any takers?" The room was silent. No one would take me up on my bet. One sarcastic colleague said, "Yeah, he'll lose the weight, even if he has to lop off an arm!" I looked straight at him and said, "That's precisely the point. It's not a question of whether or not I will lose the weight. It's only a question of how I can do it without having to lop off any limbs!" I asked again, "Any takers?" No one would bet me. There's something deep and powerful about commitment. In near silence, it speaks louder than the loudest bravado. If you are totally committed to your customer and to your personal success, you need say very little before you start to realize the success you desire. And yes, I did lose the weight.

Committing to Excellence

"The quality of a person's life is in direct proportion to their commitment to excellence, regardless of their chosen field of endeavor."—Vince Lombardi

While most of this book is focused on landing new business, it's critical that we keep the business we already have. Signing new business is getting tougher every day. There is an age-old conflict between sales and infrastructure. If the company you sell for has the very best quality and service, the lowest prices, and the greatest selection of top brands, it will sell itself. The few rare companies that fit that bill don't typically require highly compensated sales professionals. Conversely, if the salesperson represents a significant component of the package of value, he or she typically has a greater opportunity for earnings.

In these fiercely competitive times, it is indeed a rare organization that can afford to have enough staff to handle every contingency. We, as business people, are constantly being challenged to accomplish more with less in order to stay competitive and survive. In the words of famed auto racing legend Mario Andretti, "If everything is under control, you're just not going fast enough!"

Far too many salespeople dread complaints. Handled properly, complaints are a good thing. Complaints give you an opportunity to prove how much you care about your customer, differentiating yourself from your competition. Complaints can open the door to deeper, more solid relationships. No one cares how much you know until they know how much you care. What better way to prove your commitment to your customer than for them to have a problem and you fix it? I'll go so far as to say, you can't be successful if your customers never complain.

The message is clear and you can't fake it. If selling is something that you do **to** your customer, you are in it for the quick buck, not the long term. Any success you realize will be short-lived. You will eventually hit an income ceiling and staying even will be tougher and tougher every day. The job will become frustrating, and your quality of life will diminish. Conversely, if selling is something that you do **for** your customer, everything you do will take the long-term view into consideration, and your customer will feel it. Your career will be rich and rewarding, and you will exude a sense of pride and purpose. Success will feed on itself, and your quality of life will soar.

Having Fun Is Serious Business

"If you can't do what you love and you can't learn to love what you do, do something else!"—John Powers

There's an inherent paradox in the sales profession that can really bring you down. If you're not effective, it isn't any fun. If you're not having fun, you won't be effective. Life is way too short to spend most of your waking hours engaged in an activity that you dread.

Selling is a very different kind of job. A salesperson's only reason for being employed is to generate revenue. In most organizations, that's all they do, and they're the only ones who do it. Somewhere in their career, outside salespeople learn that if they're making the numbers, no one really cares how hard they're working. If they're not making the numbers, no one really cares how hard they're working! Outside sales is about productivity, not activity.

As early as your first sales call, your prospect starts to form a picture of what life will be like with you as a supplier. If that's a picture of a fun exciting place, they might just let you lead them there. If it's a dark, scary, or depressing place, forget it!

Making work fun is more critical today than ever before. Hundreds of thousands of people are being laid off, some after giving 20 or more years of faithful service to their employer. The remaining staff is forced to accomplish more with fewer resources. Frequently, those who remain watched many of their family, friends and co-workers lose their livelihoods. They may feel sad, guilty or scared about it while relieved that they're still working. They may wonder why they still remain and for just how long that will be. No longer do they worry about how long it will take to complete their tasks and how much free time will be left after they do. Today, the challenge is to prioritize what can get done and make sure that the tasks that can't get done are the least important ones. Often, the only person who really knew how to properly perform a certain task is one of the people who was laid off.

Thousands more are caught in corporate buyouts. If they're lucky, they're the ones that are left when the dust settles. Unfortunately, they have to prove their value all over again to a new set of supervisors who may or may not have the same description of how the job should be done. As if that's not bad enough, all the rules changed since 9/11. Not only was 9/11 a tremendous shock to the economy, it rocked the sheer foundation of many of our lives. Most Americans have a different perspective regarding just how vulnerable and precarious our lives really are.

Keep all of this in mind when you are talking to your prospect. Think about their picture of the future and what their life will be like. Inevitably, you'll come to the conclusion that the future is a very uncertain place. The difference between a bright outlook for the future and a bleak one is confidence, plain and simple. The days when we could pretty well count on a continuation of business as usual are long gone. Your friends, your family, your peers, your supervisor, your customers, and your prospects all want to believe that the future is bright despite negative press to the contrary. If you want to be successful, you will need to develop the confidence to take the lead. Confidence is contagious when it's real. If you are lighthearted, fun loving, serious and confident about being part of a bright future, your prospect can't help but want to be part of it as well. I'm not talking about blind naïve fun from being a goof-off. That's short lived and you'll eventually pay the price when it comes crashing down. I'm talking about the kind of fun that comes from being serious and winning.

I remember that when my daughter was small and involved in sports, we used to tell her, "Don't worry about winning or losing, just have fun out there." It didn't take long for her to figure out that the game isn't much fun if you keep losing. Winning is fun. If your prospects feel that you're having fun, they'll know that you're a winner. They too want to win so that they can have fun. If you can inspire them with the confidence that they can win, they can have fun, and you can help them to get there, you're in. Great attitudes are not the result of success, success is the result of great attitudes.

Everything changes. Nothing stands still. I'm not here to "sell" you anything. I only hope that I've given you a fresh perspective on how to approach your career and your life. Don't get frustrated if it doesn't all fit together the first time. Every piece of the puzzle interacts with other pieces. As you work on one aspect, it may not connect neatly with another. Stick with it, keep working and, most importantly, commit to your goals.

If your intentions are pure, good things will happen. Your life will get better as you make life better for your customers and your prospective customers. As you embark on your exciting new career direction, I'd like to leave you with this thought from Vince Lombardi.

"Any man's finest hour—his greatest fulfillment to all he holds dear—is that moment when he has to work his heart out in a good cause and he's exhausted on the field of battle—victorious!"

Worksheets

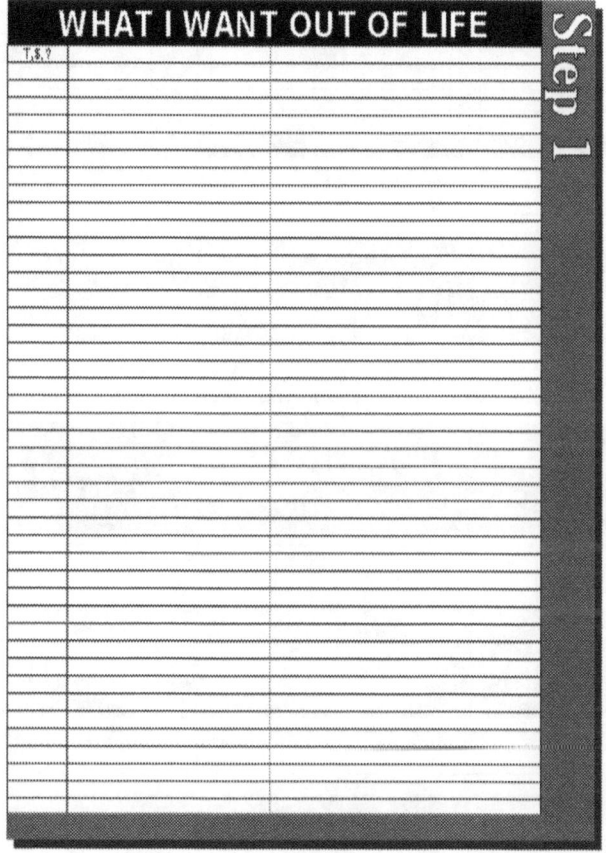

WHAT I WANT OUT OF LIFE		Step 1
T, $, ?		

Yr	A: Annual Income Goal		B: Cost of Living Adjustment		C: Additional Income Needed		D: Adjusted Income Goal
1		X	%	=		A+C=	
2		X	%	=		A+C=	
3		X	%	=		A+C=	
4		X	%	=		A+C=	
5		X	%	=		A+C=	

Step 2

Yr	A: Annual Income		B: Rate of attrition		C: Income Lost		D: Adjusted Income
1		X	%	=		A-C=	
2		X	%	=		A-C=	
3		X	%	=		A-C=	
4		X	%	=		A-C=	
5		X	%	=		A-C=	

Step 3

Adjusted income goal from step 2		Adjusted income from step 3		Additional Income Needed
	Subtract		=	

Step 4

Current Annual Commission Income			Monthly Commission Income
		Divided by 12 =	

Step 5

Adjusted income goal from step 2		Current Annual Income		Additional Income Needed
	Subtract		=	

Step 6

Additional Annual Income Needed			Monthly Commission Income Needed
		Divided by 12 =	

Step 7

Additional Monthly Income Needed			Monthly Commission Growth Needed
		Divided by 60 =	

Step 8

Step 9

Year 1

	JAN	FEB	MAR	APR	MAY	JUN	JUL	AUG	SEP	OCT	NOV	DEC
Current Monthly Income												
Projected Monthly Growth												
Projected Monthly Income												

Year 2

	JAN	FEB	MAR	APR	MAY	JUN	JUL	AUG	SEP	OCT	NOV	DEC
Current Monthly Income												
Projected Monthly Growth												
Projected Monthly Income												

Year 3

	JAN	FEB	MAR	APR	MAY	JUN	JUL	AUG	SEP	OCT	NOV	DEC
Current Monthly Income												
Projected Monthly Growth												
Projected Monthly Income												

Year 4

	JAN	FEB	MAR	APR	MAY	JUN	JUL	AUG	SEP	OCT	NOV	DEC
Current Monthly Income												
Projected Monthly Growth												
Projected Monthly Income												

Year 5

	JAN	FEB	MAR	APR	MAY	JUN	JUL	AUG	SEP	OCT	NOV	DEC
Current Monthly Income												
Projected Monthly Growth												
Projected Monthly Income												

Current Income		Number of Accounts		Avg. Income Per Account
	Divided by		=	

Step 10

Additional Income Needed		Average Income Per Account		Number of Additional Accounts Needed
	Divided by		=	

Step 11

Total hours per month spent with existing accounts		Approximate number of hours per week spent with existing accounts		Number of accounts		Hours per Week per account needed to maintain existing business
	Divided by 4 weeks	=		Divided by	=	

Step 12

Number of Existing Accounts		Number of Additional Accounts You Need		Total Number of Accounts to Maintain to Reach Income Goal		Hours per Week Per Account: Existing business		Hours You Will Spend per week Maintaining Business once Signed (not including all non-selling activities)
	+		=		X		=	

Step 13

Annual income from commission		Weekly commission income		Hours worked per Week		Your current hourly wage
	Divided by 50	=		Divided by	=	

Step 14

Annual commission income goal		Weekly commission goal		Hours worked per Week		Your hourly wage Goal
	Divided by 50 weeks	=		Divided by	=	

Step 15

Active customers by zone   Zone:

My current hourly wage is $ [   ]   Per Hour

My hourly wage objective is $ [   ]   Per Hour

A: ACTIVE CUSTOMERS Account Name	B: Commission generated per month	C: Hours spent per month maintaining	D: Hourly Wage B/C
1			
2			
3			
4			
5			
6			
7			
8			
9			
10			
11			
12			
13			
14			
15			
16			
17			
18			
19			
20			
21			
22			
23			
24			
25			
26			
27			
28			
29			
30			
TOTALS			

Prospects by zone   Zone: [   ]

My current hourly wage is $ [   ]   Per Hour

My hourly wage objective is $ [   ]   Per Hour

	A: PROSPECTS Account Name	B: Commission generated per month	C: Hours spent per month maintaining	D: Hourly Wage B/C
1				
2				
3				
4				
5				
6				
7				
8				
9				
10				
11				
12				
13				
14				
15				
16				
17				
18				
19				
20				
21				
22				
23				
24				
25				
26				
27				
28				
29				
30				
	TOTALS			

Suspect by zone		Zone:

SUSPECTS

	Account Name	City/State
1		
2		
3		
4		
5		
6		
7		
8		
9		
10		
11		
12		
13		
14		
15		
16		
17		
18		
19		
20		
21		
22		
23		
24		
25		
26		
27		
28		
29		
30		
31		
32		
33		
34		
35		
36		
37		
38		
39		
40		

0-595-32688-9